My Disney STARS AND HEROES 4

Student's Book with eBook

Mary Roulston

Scope and Sequence

Meet our Stars and Heroes!
page 4

Character introductions
She's good at …
He always …
She enjoys …
Can you …? Are you …?

Stars and Heroes song
I have …
I am …
I enjoy …
Do I …?

	Vocabulary	Grammar and communication	Personal and Social Skills	Cross-curricular	Project and strategies
1 Competition time page 10 	**Actions in a competition** Actions in a race / Obstacles on a racetrack	Ralph always wrecks the building. I go through a tunnel every day. We're cheering the winner. I'm finishing the race now. **Make suggestions (designing a racetrack)** You could go around the hill. We could race through the tunnel.	**Self-awareness:** Loving myself / Mistakes help me learn. I am proud of / believe in myself. I am ready to learn. **Story:** Sports day	**Technology:** Computer codes *algorithm, bug, conditional, instructions, loop*	**Project:** A racetrack game **Collaboration:** Sharing ideas and making group decisions.
2 Let's celebrate page 22 	**Things in the town center** Things at festivals / Describing festivals	Where were the people? They were in the street. Why were the people in the street? Because there was a parade. When was the parade? It was at ten o'clock. **Talk about a festival (poster)** Was it awful? No, it wasn't. Were they noisy? Yes, they were.	**Self-management:** Thinking before acting / Don't rush in. Count to ten. Stop and think. Make good choices. **Story:** The festival parade	**Science:** States of matter *condensation, evaporation, freeze, melt, water vapor*	**Project:** A festival blog **Self-management:** Writing clear notes
3 Let's get active! page 34 	**Sports activities** More sports / Adverbs	He's good at trampolining. I'm not very good at skateboarding yet. I want to learn! **Ask and answer about activities (game cards)** She's playing badminton well. They're snowboarding safely. He's cheering happily.	**Self-awareness:** Motivating myself / I'm not good at roller skating yet. I want to learn. I can get better! **Story:** Eleni's gymnastics journal	**Science:** Blood and circulation *blood, blood vessels, brain, heart, oxygen, pump*	**Project:** A sports journal **Presentation skills:** describing images and actions
4 Amazing animals page 46 	**Animals** Describing animals / More animals	A rabbit is cuter than a snake. A buffalo is hairier than a frog. A hippo is bigger than an otter. **Make comparisons about animals (cards)** I think wolves are the fiercest animals. Blue whales are the largest animals on Earth.	**Responsible decision-making:** Recognizing stereotypes / Most people think that … Why do you think that? I think that, too. **Story:** The zoo	**Science:** Biomes *aquatic, climate, rainforest, species, tundra*	**Project:** An animal display **Self-management:** Researching and organizing information
5 In the past page 58 	**Things from the past** Actions in the past / More things from the past	She carried fruit. We didn't farm. **Ask and answer about ancient cultures (questionnaires)** Did they live in huts? No, they didn't. Did they use baskets? Yes, they did.	**Social awareness:** Appreciating diversity and celebrating cultures / I think your culture is interesting. That sounds fun! **Story:** Grandma's story	**Engineering:** Ships and forces *anchor, float, push, pull, sails, sink*	**Project:** A class culture book **Collaboration:** Respectful decision-making

Welcome
page 6

Ordinal numbers	What's the date on Friday? It's the 24th.	Relationship skills:
Months and dates	When's your birthday? It's November 6th.	Being brave
		Be brave and make a friend with someone new.

	Vocabulary	Grammar and communication	Personal and Social Skills	Cross-curricular	Project and strategies
6 Adventure time page 70 	**Outdoor activities** Outdoor activities More outdoor activities	I went mountain biking. I didn't go mountain biking. She got lost in the forest. She didn't get lost in the forest. **Ask and answer about adventures (outdoor activity lists)** What did she do? She went mountain biking. She didn't find a fossil.	**Relationship skills:** Building relationships I'm sorry we argued. I'm sorry I didn't listen. Let's talk about it. **Story:** Ezra's camp blog	**Science:** Living and non-living things breathe air, nutrients reproduce, roots	**Project:** An outdoors scrapbook **Presentation skills:** Good presenter behavior
7 Beach vacation page 82 	**Things on an island** Beach vacation activities More beach vacation activities	I'm going to go on vacation this summer. We're going to make a coconut cake. They aren't going to paddle in the ocean. He isn't going to stay in a hotel. **Talk about vacations (online survey)** What are you going to do in the summer? I'm going to go on vacation. Is she going to learn to surf? Yes, she is.	**Social awareness:** Understanding other people's points of view I think / want to … because … What about you? I understand why you feel that way. **Story:** The perfect vacation	**Science:** Oceans, tides and waves gravity, fall, high tide, low tide, rise, wave	**Project:** A vacation collage **Collaboration:** Making group lists
8 Awesome cities page 94 	**Places in a city** Describing cities Things in cities	I think old buildings are more beautiful than modern buildings. Rome is less modern than Shanghai. **Compare cities (fact cards)** Roof gardens are the most beautiful green spaces in cities. Universities are sometimes the least historic buildings in cities.	**Self-management:** Planning and organisational skills Let's plan. What are we going to do? What should we do first? First, / Then we could … **Story:** The city design competition	**Design:** Cities bicycle lane, city planner, environment, overpass, sustainable, transportation system	**Project:** A pop-up city map **Self-management:** Making lists of what to include. Using pictures to remember words.
9 One planet page 106 	**Things you throw out** Good / bad things for the planet Actions to help the planet	You must recycle cans and plastic bottles. We can't waste electricity. I'm not allowed to throw plastic bottles in the trash. **Giving reasons for helping the planet (playing cards)** We can recycle more cans so that there is less trash. We must use cars less so that we reduce pollution.	**Responsible decision-making:** Making a difference I think we must … We could … **Story:** Carla's penpal	**Science:** Garbage biodegrade, biodegradable, burn, die, landfill, non-biodegradable	**Project:** A picture diary **Presentation skills:** Using cue cards

Grammar reference and Picture dictionary pages 118–127

Meet our Stars and Heroes!

1. 💬 Look. Do you know any of our Stars and Heroes?
2. 🎧 💬 Listen and point. Then play *Who am I?*

> Can you swim well?
> Yes, I can.
> Are you Moana?
> No, I'm not. Guess again!

Barley — W

Barley is brave. He has a brother named Ian. He loves history and board games.

Which birthday is his brother Ian celebrating?

Wreck-It Ralph — 1

Ralph is nice, but he usually wrecks things. He's a good friend to Vanellope.

What does Vanellope give Ralph?

Anna — 2

Anna is very caring. She always helps people. Her sister is Elsa.

Why was Anna excited at the start of the video story?

Riley — 3

Riley is a quiet girl. We see five emotions inside her head! She's good at ice hockey.

What isn't Riley very good at?

Nick Wilde — 4

Nick is a smart fox. Judy is his friend. They're a good team.

Which animal says Judy Hopps is cute?

Pocahontas — 5

Pocahontas is brave and smart. She's good at swimming and running fast.

How did Pocahontas travel to London?

Queen Elinor 6

Queen Elinor has a daughter named Merida. Elinor is tall and strong. She doesn't like adventures.

What animal did Queen Elinor change into?

Moana 7

Moana lives on an island. She's friendly and brave. She enjoys collecting shells.

What is Moana going to do in her boat?

Baymax 8

Baymax is a robot. He takes care of people. His best friend is Hiro.

Which imaginary city do Baymax and Hiro live in?

WALL-E 9

WALL-E is a friendly robot. He has a friend named EVE. He picks up garbage to make the Earth cleaner.

What must EVE find?

Sing-along

3 **Listen and sing.**

Hello, Disney Friends!
Hello, everyone!
Welcome, Disney Friends!
Let's all have some fun!

Let's travel to new places.
And meet new people, too.
Let's have some great adventures.
We're ready! How about you?

Chorus

5 Find answers to the questions as you work through the book.

4 Complete and write a question for you. Ask a friend.

Me! _____

I have _____ .
I am _____ .
I enjoy _____ .
My favorite Disney friend is _____ .
Do I _____ ?

5

Welcome!

LESSON 1 Ordinal numbers

1 🎧 0.3 Listen, match, and say.

1st 2nd 3rd 4th 5th 6th 7th 8th 9th 10th

| ninth | fourth | seventh | tenth | sixth | third | first | fifth | second | eighth |

2 ▶ OA Watch the video. What's the date of Ian's birthday?

3 ▶ OA Watch again and answer.

  1. Why does Ian find it hard to make friends?
  2. When do you feel shy?

4 💬 Play *Say the date*.   on (Tuesday)   yesterday   today   tomorrow

What was the date on Monday?   It was the 21st.

I can name dates.

6

LESSON 2 Months and dates

1 🎧 0.4 **Listen and say.** January February March April May June July August September October November December

2 🎧 0.5 **Listen and write.**

 What's the date today?   ¹_____ October ²_____ .

Oh, no! ³_____ my dad's birthday ⁴_____ . I always forget it!

3 🎵 0.6 **Listen, chant, and act.**

January, February, March, April, May,
When's his birthday?
June, July, August, September,
October, November, December?
I can't remember!

4 💬 **Use a calendar. Ask and answer.**

What's the date?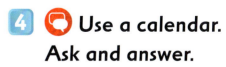

It's February 13th.

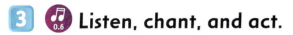
I can ask and answer about the date.

LESSON 3
When's your birthday?

1 🎧 0.7 💬 **Listen, read, and match. Then say.**

① "When's your birthday?" she asks.

② "My birthday is on April 18th. It's today!" he says.

a

b

2 🎧 0.8 **Listen and match.**

1

2

3

4

a JULY 31

b DECEMBER 17

c JANUARY 2

d MAY 23

3 💬 **When's your birthday? Write the month and circle. Then ask and answer.**

1	2	3	4	5	6	7	8	9	10	11
12	13	14	15	16	17	18	19	20	21	22
23	24	25	26	27	28	29	30	31		

When's your birthday?

It's June 19th.

Story ▶▶▶ **Find the children in the story. Which children do you think are new?**

ALEX

Carla

Eleni

EZRA

Kai

I can ask and answer about birthdays.

New friends!

LESSON 4
What's the date?

1 🎧 **Listen and read. Who feels shy?**

① I'm Alex and this is my sister, Eleni. It's our first day at Park School.
"Hi," says Carla. "Are you both in Fourth Grade? Are you twins?"
"No, we're not twins," I say, "My birthday is September 3rd."
"When's your birthday, Eleni?" Ezra asks.
Eleni doesn't answer. She feels shy.
"Her birthday is August 16th," I say.

② "What's the date today?" I ask Carla.
"Look," says Carla, "It's March 11th. It's on the board."
"I can't read it. I'm visually impaired," I say.
"Oh, can't you see?" asks Carla.
"Yes, I can see, but things aren't very clear. I can read very big writing. I have special books, too. I feel the words!"

③ "What do you like doing, Alex?" asks Ezra.
"I like skateboarding, running, and reading," I say.
"Wow! Is this Eleni?" asks Kai, picking up a photo.
"Can you show us, Eleni?" asks Kai.

④ Eleni looks up. She's starting to feel brave because Ezra, Kai, and Carla are nice. She does a perfect cartwheel.
"Wow. Can you teach us?" they ask.
"Sure!" says Eleni. I like my new school and friends. Eleni does, too!

Be brave.

2 **Read again and write.**

① It's Alex and Eleni's _____ day at Park School.
② The children are in _____ Grade.
③ Eleni's birthday is _____ .
④ The day's date is _____ .

3 💬 **Look at the writing Alex can feel. Write the dates. Then ask and answer.**

⠁ ⠃ ⠉ ⠙ ⠑ ⠋ ⠛ ⠓ ⠊ ⠚
1 2 3 4 5 6 7 8 9 10

April ⠙ _____
October ⠉ _____
July ⠛ _____
January ⠑ _____

What's that date?

It's April 8th.

I can ask and answer about dates.

1 Competition time

Do you take part in competitions? Share ideas.

cross the finish line

video story

1 🔘 1A Watch the video. Check (✓). Who gets a medal?

 1
 2
 3

2 🔘 1A Watch again and answer.

1. What doesn't Ralph like about himself?
2. Why is Vanellope sad?
3. What does Ralph learn about himself?

LESSON 1 Vocabulary

3 🎧 Listen, find, and say. Then tell a friend.

4 🎵 Listen, chant, and act.

> It's competition time!
> We're on the starting line,
>
> Let's start the race!
> Let's race the cars,
> Enjoy taking part!
>
> It's competition time!
> Cross the finish line.
>
> You can walk, or drive, or run.
> Win a trophy, get a medal,
> Come and have some fun!

win a trophy

5 💬 Act out and play *Guess the action*.

Are you getting a medal?

No, I'm not. I'm winning a trophy!

Talk buddies

start a race

get a medal

I can name actions in a competition.

LESSON 2
Vocabulary

1 🎧 1.3 **Listen and say. Then tell a friend.**

 1 wear a helmet
 2 win a prize
 3 score points
 4 fall over
 5 lose a race
 6 take part
 7 go through a tunnel
 8 cheer for the winner

2 🎧 1.4 **Listen and say the action.**

3 Read and match. Then write.

1. These are the prizes the winners get.
2. Oh, no! There's a problem. She can't win now.
3. Yes! Five more points for our team!

Guess what?
US swimmer Michael Phelps has 23 Olympic gold medals.

a
_____
lose a race

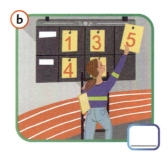
b
_____

c
_____

4 💬 **Imagine you are watching a race. Talk about what you see.**

They're wearing helmets. They're starting the race …

They're going through a tunnel …

Talk buddies

I can name actions in a race.

12

LESSON 3
Grammar

1 🎧 1.5 **Listen, read, and circle.**

1. This is Felix. Felix always **is getting** / **gets** a medal.
2. Vanellope **is racing** / **races** a car now.

2 🎧 1.6 **Listen and write E (Eleni) or K (Kai). Listen again. Write one action they are not doing.**

1. doing homework ☐ ☐
2. playing a racing game ☐ ☐
3. starting a race ☐ ☐
4. coming home from school ☐ ☐
5. riding a bike ☐ ☐
6. going through a tunnel ☐ ☐

Grammar Heroes
Routines
Ralph **always wrecks** the building.
I **go** through a tunnel **every day**.
Now
We**'re cheering** for the winner.
I**'m finishing** the race **now**.

ⓐ Eleni isn't _____ .
ⓑ Kai _____ .

3 Complete for you.

Now:
I'm _____
I'm _____
Every day:
I _____
I _____

4 💬 **Look at 3 and share ideas.**

I eat lunch every day.
Me too!

I always wake up at seven.
Not me!

Talk buddies

I can talk about routine activities and things happening now.

LESSON 4
Story

Sports day

1 Look. What type of race is it?

2 Listen and read. Who wins the race on sports day?

① It's school sports day next week. I can run fast – I want to get a medal this year. We start the practice race. The white lines are really clear, so I can see them. Ezra is next to me.

② Ezra doesn't usually run fast, but he's running fast today. Oh, no! Ezra is falling over. I'm falling over, too!
"I'm sorry, Alex," says Ezra, "I'm so clumsy. I hate it!"
"Don't worry! It was a mistake."

③ The next day Ezra comes to my house, "I'm sorry about yesterday, Alex. Are you hurt?"
"No, I'm fine," I say, "Are you hurt?"
"Yes, I can't take part in sports day," says Ezra, "I hate being clumsy!"
"I can't see very well," I say, "I don't always like it, but I think more about the things I *do* like about myself. I like being a fast runner and winning races. But I can't race in video games."
"I can help you play," says Ezra.

Think!
Which game is Alex playing?
Go to to page 119 to find out!

④ Ezra tells me where to go in a racing game: "Go around that tree! Now go straight – you're going through a tunnel…" He's great! I finish the race – I don't usually finish! Then I have an idea. I know how Ezra can take part in sports day…

⑤ I'm starting the race on sports day. I can hear Ezra's voice. "Kai is running fast, but here comes Alex. He's crossing the finish line! Alex wins!"

My friends and family are cheering, and Ezra is cheering, too. He's enjoying taking part in sports day!

3 Read again and write answers.

1. What happens in the practice race?

2. What does Ezra help Alex do?
   _____

3. Does Ezra take part in sports day?
   _____

4. How does he take part?
   _____

4 Think and answer.

1. Why is Ezra angry with himself in the practice race?
2. What two things does Alex say he likes about himself?
3. How many different ways do you think Alex helps Ezra?

5 💬 Act out the story. Then reflect.

Reflect
How can you help your friend like themselves more?

I like being a fast runner and winning races. But I can't race in video games.

I can help you play.

I can read a story about finding self-acceptance.

15

LESSON 5
Vocabulary and Grammar

1 🎧 1.8 **Listen and say. Then tell a friend.**

 1 into the net

 2 along the racetrack

 3 around the cones

 4 across the bridge

 5 over the hill

 6 past the flags

Ways to learn
Act out the movements with your school equipment.

2 🎧 1.9 **Listen, read, and draw the route.**

Ezra: Hey Carla, what are you doing?

Carla: I'm drawing an idea for a racetrack for the school sports day. The winning idea gets a prize!

Ezra: Can I help?

Carla: Sure. Look, you start the race and run ten meters, then you go around five cones. Next, you go over this net …

Ezra: What if people fall over? You could go under the net …

Carla: Great idea!

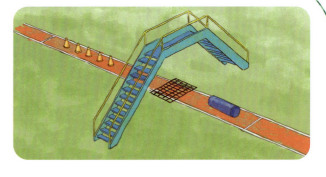

Ezra: You could go over something else.

Carla: Yes! I know – you could go over a bridge. And then you could go through a tunnel.

Ezra: And then cross the finish line!

Carla: Perfect!

Grammar Heroes
You **could go** around the hill.
We **could race** through the tunnel.

3 💬 **Share ideas for your school sports day.**

 We could have a running race.

 We could race in teams.

Talk buddies

I can talk about movements and make suggestions.

LESSON 6
Listening and Speaking

1 Watch the video and choose.

1. Who isn't at the start of the race?
   - a) Vanellope
   - b) King Candy
2. What happens when Vanellope comes out of the tunnel?
   - a) she goes around a hill
   - b) she flies through the air
3. How does Vanellope escape King Candy?
   - a) she uses her coding bug
   - b) she goes out of the tunnel

2 Listen and draw arrows → ↑ ↓ ←. Then number the instructions in order.

go across the bridge ☐
go along to the finish line and past the flags ☐
go down and over the candy ☐
go through the hill ☐
go up and around the volcano ☐
start the race ☐ 1
go down and past the cake ☐

Let's communicate!

3 Design a racetrack with a friend. Then write instructions.

Go online — Communication Kit

We could have a racetrack in a house!

Yes! You could go over a bed and under a sofa.

I can use a racetrack to make suggestions.

17

LESSON 7
Myself and others

Loving myself

1 Lessons 1 and 4   **Think and write R (Ralph) or E (Ezra).**

What they don't like
a) I'm clumsy. ☐
b) I'm the bad guy. ☐

What they learn
c) I'm nice and they need me in the game. ☐
d) I'm a good friend and good at other things, too. ☐

2 **Read and match. Then share ideas.**

1. I always make mistakes.
2. I fail exams – I'm stupid.
3. I don't like myself.

a) There are lots of things I like about myself.
b) I can learn from my mistakes.
c) It's OK not to know everything – I can study more.

3 **Complete for you.**

An unhelpful way you think about yourself: _____

A helpful way to think: _____

Useful Language
Mistakes help me learn.
I am proud of / believe in myself.
I am ready to learn.

4 **Look at 3. Write a note to help you love yourself more.**

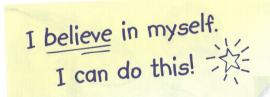

Be a hero!
Tell a friend your favorite things about them.

You make me smile.

18   **Self-awareness** I can recognize ways to love myself.

Computer codes

LESSON 8
My world

1 🅿️ **Watch the video and circle.**

Bugs / Codes tell a computer game what to do.

2 🎧 **Explore** Read, listen, and circle.

Coding

Algorithms
Codes tell your computer how to do something. There are two types of code. **Algorithms** are one type of code. Algorithms are **instructions**. When Ralph wrecks a building, that is because of the code. Every move up and across the building is a line of code. It could look like this:

Loops
Sometimes, algorithms are very long, but a **loop** is short. It's the same instruction, but it is short because it tells the computer how many times to do the same thing. An algorithm without a loop could look like this: ↓↓↓↓. The same algorithm with a loop looks like this: 4×(↓). Both tell Ralph: "Move down four times!"

a. A mistake in the code is a **conditional / bug**.
b. A yes/no decision in the code is a **conditional / loop**.
c. Code or instructions is an **algorithm / bug**.
d. A short code is a **loop / algorithm**.

Conditionals
Conditional codes help a computer make yes/no decisions. Imagine Vanellope racing her car. She comes to a tunnel. Conditional code tells her to go into the tunnel. This is a simple conditional code from Ralph's game:

| Is Ralph in front of the building? | → Yes → | Start wrecking! |
| | → No → | Continue walking. |

Bugs
Codes can have a mistake, which is called a **bug**. For example, an algorithm to go along a straight racetrack looks like this: →→→. The same algorithm with a bug looks like this: →↑→.

Try it!
Write a code for how you go from your classroom to the school playground.

3 💡 **Think** Complete the conditional code.

Go across the finish line.   Go along the racetrack. (x2)   Go into the tunnel.

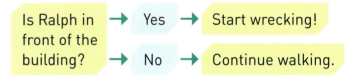

I can read and understand about coding.

19

LESSON 9 Project

A racetrack game

1 🎧 1.12 (Review) Listen. Then complete the key and draw the route.

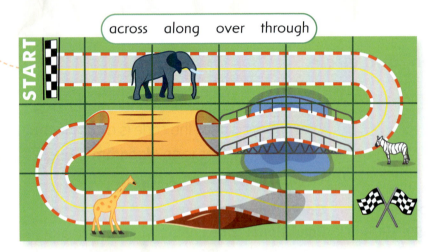

across   along   over   through

Key

1 ⟶ Go _____ the racetrack.
2 ⌐→ Go _____ the bridge.
3 ⊖⊖→ Go _____ the tunnel.
4 ⤵ Go _____ the hill.

2 💬 (Get ready) In groups, share your ideas.

What type of race do you want to do?

What obstacles are there in your race?

What could you do at the obstacles?

We could have a *bike* race.

The racers could go *around cones*.

Tips
Collaboration
- ☐ Write down all of the ideas and discuss them.
- ☐ Vote by putting your hands up.
- ☐ Include as many different group members' ideas as you can.

3 (Create) Vote on your ideas and design your racetrack. Then write instructions as code. *Workbook* page 13

Writing: code
- Draw instruction pictures for your race and write a key.
- Use action words: **Climb** over the net. **Go** around the cones.

4 💬 (Share) Share your racetrack with the class.

20   I can create a racetrack game.

LESSON 10
Review

I can do it!

1 🎧 1.13 **Read, write, and match. Then listen and check.**

① This is Ralph's game. Felix **1** _____ (get) a medal every game. Look – he **2** _____ (get) a medal now. Ralph never **3** _____ (get) a medal or **4** _____ (win) a trophy.

② This is Vanellope's game. She **1** _____ usually **2** _____ (not race). But now Vanellope **3** _____ (cross) the finish line.

Movie challenge
How many actions in Vanellope's race can you say?

a ☐   b ☐

2 💬 **Write about playing a car racing game. Then tell a friend.**

cross the finish line   get a medal   go along the racetrack   go around a cupcake
go into the tunnel   score points   ~~start the race~~   wear a helmet   win a trophy

I'm starting the race. I'm wearing a ... _____
_____

I can ...
- 💬 name and identify actions in a race ☐
- 📖 read a story ☐
- 🎨 design a racetrack game ☐
- 🔍 find ways to love myself ☐

Sticker time

✅ **I completed Unit 1!**

Extra Lesson   Go online Big Project

2 Let's celebrate!

What do you celebrate? How? Share ideas.

palace

Video story

1. Watch the video. Number in order.

   a   b   c

2. Watch again and answer.

   1. Who was Anna's best friend?
   2. Does Anna think before she says "yes" to Hans?
   3. Elsa is angry and scared. What does she do?

LESSON 1 Vocabulary

people

town square

3 🎧 2.1 **Listen, find, and say. Then tell a friend.**

1	2	3	4

4 🎵 2.2 **Listen, chant, and act.**

There was a celebration,
Lots of people were there.
The celebration was in the palace,
And in the town square.

There were decorations around the fountain,
There was dancing in the square.
I was very happy,
Because all my friends were there.

5 💬 **Say what you can see. Then describe your town center.**

Elsa is near the fountain. There are lots of fountains in my town. There's a fountain in the town square.

Talk buddies

fountain

I can name things in the town center.

23

LESSON 2
Vocabulary

1 🎧 2.3 Listen and say. Then tell a friend.

1 fireworks

2 float

3 parade

4 festival

5 costume

6 traditional food

7 stall

8 lantern

2 🎧 2.4 Listen and say a festival word.

3 Look, read, and complete with words from 1.

Guess what?
At the Lantern Floating Festival in Hawaii, the lanterns go on the ocean!

1 There is one _____ in the parade.
2 The people are wearing _____ .
3 There are _____ in the sky.
4 The stall is selling _____ .

4 💬 Write three sentences about a festival. Then play *Draw my picture*.

It's a festival. ...

It's a festival. There are pink and red fireworks in the sky. There are children in animal costumes.

Talk buddies

I can name things at festivals.

LESSON 3
Grammar

1 🎧 2.5 **Listen, read, and complete.**

1. Where was the flower _____?

2. The flower stall was in the _____.

2 🎧 2.6 **Listen and choose.**

1. The treasure hunt was …
   a. after the parade   b. before the parade
2. The treasure was …
   a. lanterns   b. toys
3. The treasure was …
   a. in the palace   b. in the fountain

Grammar Heroes
Where were the people?
They **were** in the street.
Why were the people in the street?
Because there **was** a parade.
When was the parade?
It **was** at ten o'clock.

3 **Put the words in order to make questions.**

1. treasure hunt / was / When / the / ? _____
2. was / the / treasure / What / ? _____
3. the / were / Where / toys / ? _____

4 💬 **Read the invitation. Then close your books and play *Memory*!**

School Party
In the sports center on Friday 8th at six o'clock.
This year, the costume theme is animals.
Activities: costume making, lantern making, a parade, and fireworks.
Bring some money! There are candy stalls and toy stalls.

Where was the school party?

It was in the sports center.

Talk buddies

I can ask questions about things in the past.

25

LESSON 4
Story

The festival parade

1 Look. What's happening? Where is Kai at the start of the story?

2 🎧 2.7 Listen and read. How does Kai find the parade?

It was the day of the town festival. Kai's class was on a float in the parade. His costume was ready! "Hurry up!" says his dad. "What time is the parade?" "It was at seven o'clock last year," says Kai.

Kai arrives in the town square, but the parade isn't there. He hears two people talking: "The parade was amazing!" says the man. "Excuse me," says Kai, "Where was the parade?" "It was near the fountain," says the woman. "When was it there?" asks Kai. "It was there at 6:30," she answers.

Decision Time! **Option 1:** Run to the fountain. **Option 2:** Stop and think.

Kai runs to the fountain, but the parade isn't there. Lots of people are walking away. He's late!

Decision time! **Option 1:** Run in the opposite direction to where he was. **Option 2:** Stop and think.

Kai is running all over town. He is lost! His cell phone rings and it's his mom. "Kai, the parade was in our street. I was so excited to see you, but you weren't there! Where were you?"

Decision time! **Option 1:** Run home. **Option 2:** Stop and think.

Think! Can you number the route of the parade in order? Go to to page 120 to find out!

Kai runs to his street, but the parade isn't there. Then he sees fireworks in the sky. His phone rings and it's Carla. "Where were you? Where are you now?" she asks.
"I was late. Now I'm lost," says Kai.

Kai stops and listens. The parade is noisy! He follows the sound. Then he sees colorful lanterns on floats. Kai finds the parade next to the park.

"Kai!" calls Carla, "You're here!"

"Let's enjoy the fireworks!" says Ezra.

"And the traditional food!" says Kai, "I'm hungry!"

3 Read again and write answers.

1. Where was the parade at 6:30?
   _____
2. Was Kai's mom on the float?
   _____
3. Where were Kai's friends?
   _____
4. What was in the sky at the end of the parade?
   _____

4 Think and answer.

1. What happens in Option 1? Why?
2. What happens in Option 2? Why?
3. What do you do to make a decision? Why?

5 Act out the story. Then reflect.

Reflect
What happens when you stop and think?

I was late. Now I'm lost.

Kai! You're here!

I can read a story about thinking before acting.

27

LESSON 5
Vocabulary and Grammar

1 🎧 2.8 **Listen and say. Then tell a friend.**

 1 amazing

 2 colorful

 3 fun

 4 awful

 5 noisy

 6 scary

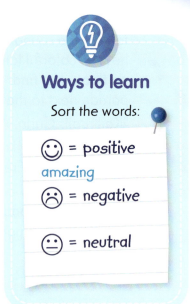

Ways to learn

Sort the words:

☺ = positive
amazing

☹ = negative

😐 = neutral

2 🎧 2.9 **Listen, read, and check (✔).**

Ezra: I was sick last week, so I wasn't at the school play. I was very sad to miss it.
Carla: Oh, no!
Ezra: Were you there? How was the school play?
Carla: Yes, I was. It was amazing!
Ezra: Were the costumes colorful?
Carla: No, they weren't. They were black and white.
Ezra: Was it fun?
Carla: Yes, it was. It was scary, too!
Ezra: Was it noisy?
Carla: Yes, it was! It was very noisy.

Grammar Heroes
Was it awful?
No, it **wasn't**.
Were they noisy?
Yes, they **were**.

3 💬 **Look at 2. Play *Guess the picture*.**

Were the costumes colorful?

No, they weren't.

Picture 2?

 Talk buddies

I can describe festivals.   Go online Phonics

LESSON 6
Listening and Speaking

1 ▶ Watch the video and choose.

1. How does Freya describe the celebration?
   - a exciting
   - b amazing
   - c scary
2. Who was at the celebration?
   - a Anna
   - b Elsa
   - c Kaye
3. What was the weather like?
   - a cold
   - b rainy
   - c sunny

2 🎧 Listen and complete the poster for the festival.

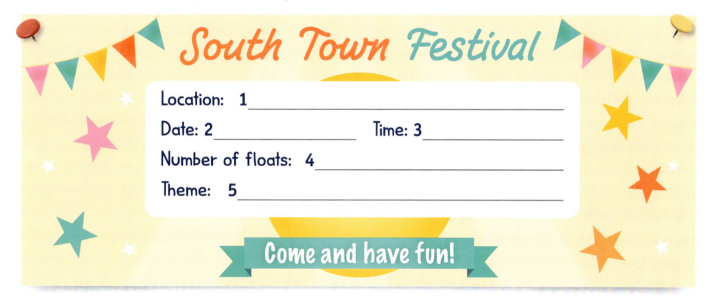

Let's communicate!

3 💬 Make your poster. Then ask and answer.

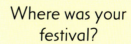
Go online
Communication Kit

Where was your festival?

It was in the palace.

I can use a festival poster to talk about past events.

LESSON 7
Myself and others

Think before you act!

1 Lessons 1 and 4 2A 💡 Think and match. Why don't they stop and think?

 1
 2
 3

a) He/She is scared or angry. ☐
b) He/She is late and worried ☐
c) He/She does things for love. ☐

2 💡 💬 Complete the questionnaire. Then share your answers.

Are you impulsive?

1 Your teacher tells you about a school festival. Do you …
  a) say you want to take part?
  b) wait to see what your friends do?

2 Your teacher has a box of costumes for the festival. Do you …
  a) take the first costume you see?
  b) look for a costume you like?

3 You see a toy you like at a festival stall. Do you …
  a) buy the toy?
  b) look and see how much money you have?

4 Is making a very quick decision …
  a) exciting?
  b) OK sometimes?

My answers = Mostly As ◯   Mostly Bs ◯

3 🎧 2.11 Look at 2. Think and match. Then listen and check.

❶ Mostly As   ☐ You stop and think and make good choices – good job!
❷ Mostly Bs   ☐ You are very impulsive. Stop and think a little more.

4 Give advice to a friend to help them stop and think.

Useful Language
Don't rush in.
Count to ten.
Stop and think.
Make good choices.

Imagine your friend wants to go to a party, but she doesn't tell her parents.
What can you say?

Be a hero!
Write a list of things to help you think before you act.

30   **Self-management** I can think before I act.

States of matter

LESSON 8
My world

1 Watch the video and circle.

Which of these things are water?
air / ice / sunlight / water vapor / wind

2 **Explore** Read, listen, and circle.

a Ice / water vapor is in the air.   b Liquid / Melting is when ice changes back to water.

Ice, water, and water vapor

Water all around
Look around you. Can you see any water? How does water feel? Water feels wet – it's a liquid. There is water around us we can't always see. Where is it? It's in the air. This water is called **water vapor**. What about water in cold places? That water is very cold and hard. It's called ice.

Freezing
On Earth we usually see water as a liquid. It's in rivers, lakes, and oceans. It's the water we use to drink and wash. When it gets very cold, water changes into ice. This change is called **freezing**. Ice is cold and hard. Do you go ice skating?

Melting
When it gets hot again, ice changes back into water. This is called **melting**. Do you put ice in your drinks on hot days? Do you eat ice cream? Do you see it melting?

Evaporation and condensation
When water gets very, very hot, it changes into water vapor. This is called **evaporation**. Water vapor turns back into liquid water when it's cold. This is called **condensation**. Breathe on a window – you can see the condensation.

Try it!
Put some ice cubes in a warm place and watch how they melt.

3 **Think** Read again. Then write and color.

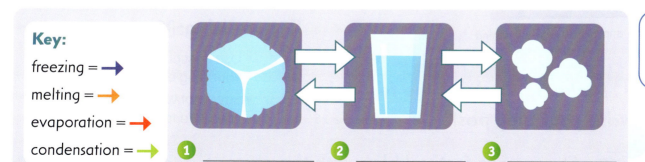

Key:
freezing = →
melting = →
evaporation = →
condensation = →

1 _____ 2 _____ 3 _____

ice
liquid water
water vapor

I can read and understand about states of matter.

31

LESSON 9
Project

A festival blog

1 🎧 2.13 (Review) Listen. How many questions does the class ask? Then listen again and write.

Festivals

There were lots of **1** _____ at the festival. It was very **2** _____ . People were in dragon **3** _____ . It wasn't **4** _____ . There were lanterns and **5** _____ in the sky.

💬 5 ♥ 20

💬 3 ♥ 18 🔁 6

2 (Get ready) Imagine you were at one of these festivals. Work with a friend to answer the questions.

- How do you feel?
- What can you see and hear?
- What words describe it?

The Rio Carnival, Brazil

Obon Festival of Lanterns, Japan

Harbin Ice and Snow Festival, China

Tips
Self-management

☐ In your notes, use different colors and pictures to help you remember the words.

☐ Choose categories for organizing your ideas, for example, what you can see, smell, and hear.

✏️ **Writing: blog**

- Use describing words to make your blog exciting.
- Say what was there and where you were to create a picture.

3 (Create) Make notes about the festival and write your blog post. Workbook page 25

4 💬 (Share) Share your festival blog with the class.

I can create a blog about a festival.

32

LESSON 10 Review

I can do it!

1 🎧 Read, listen, and circle.

A: The festival was **1 amazing / exciting**!
B: Was it **2 noisy / colorful**?
A: **3 No, it wasn't. / Yes, it was.**
B: What was the theme?
A: The theme was **4 ice / water**.

B: Was it **5 warm / cold**?
A: Yes, it was. There were ice sculptures in the **6 fountain / town square**.
B: Cool!
A: Yes, it was! Brrrrr!

2 💬 Write about the festival in the video in Lesson 6. Then ask and answer.

amazing   celebration   fountains   parades
scary   town square

Movie challenge
How many words can you say to describe the festivals in *Frozen*.

Where was the celebration?

The celebration was in the town square.

It was an **1**_____ day! It wasn't **2**_____ !
There was a **3**_____ . It was in the
4_____ . There were lots of **5**_____ .
There weren't any **6**_____ .

I can ...

- 💬 talk about festivals in the past ☐
- 📖 read a story ☐
- 🎨 write a festival blog ☐
- 🌱 think before I act ☐

Sticker time

✓ **I completed Unit 2!**

3 Let's get active!

What sports do you play? Share ideas.

playing ice hockey

hitting a puck

Video story

trampolining

1 Watch the video. Check (✓). Who makes Riley happy?

1   2   3   4

2 Watch again and answer.

1. How many emotions does Riley have in her head?
2. What is Riley not very good at?
3. What do you think Riley does to make new friends?

34

LESSON 1 **Vocabulary**

3 🎧 Listen, find, and say. Then tell a friend.

4 🎵 Listen, chant, and act.

Every weekend, I play sports!
At the ice rink,
On the trampoline.
Playing ice hockey on the team.
I'm hitting the puck!
Good luck, good luck!
Ice skating and trampolining with my friend.
I love the weekend!

5 💬 Think of activities. Then play *Sentence chain*.

I'm ice skating.

I'm ice skating and playing the guitar.

Talk buddies

ice skating

I can name sports activities.

35

LESSON 2
Vocabulary

1 🎧 3.3 **Listen and say. Then tell a friend.**

 1 snowboarding
 2 doing gymnastics
 3 cycling
 4 skateboarding

 5 roller skating
 6 playing baseball
7 playing badminton
 8 playing tennis

2 🎧 3.4 **Listen and say the activity.**

3 **Look, read, and match. Then write sentences.**

1. I'm in the park. I'm using my legs. I have special boots.
2. I'm on a team. I'm hitting the ball. I'm running.
3. I'm outside. It's cold and snowy. I'm going down a hill fast!.
4. I'm alone. I have a board. I'm pushing with my feet. I'm going fast.

Guess what?
Sherman Poppen made the first snowboard in 1965. He called it the Snurfer!

a
b
c
d

I'm playing baseball. _____ _____ _____

4 💬 **Write about the activities in 1. Then play *Guess the activity*.**

Talk buddies

I'm not on a team.
I can't play alone.
I'm hitting a ball.

I'm not on a team. I can't play alone. I'm hitting a ball.

Are you playing tennis?

36 I can name sports.

LESSON 3
Grammar

1 🎧 3.5 **Listen, read, and match.**

1. Riley is little. She isn't very good at skating yet.

2. Riley is really good at ice skating now.

a b

Grammar Heroes

He's **good at** trampolining.
I'm **not very good at** skateboarding **yet**. I want to learn!

2 🎧 3.6 **Listen and check (✔). What are they good at?**

	Carla	Ezra
1 ice hockey	○	○
2 ice skating	○	○
3 roller skating	○	○
4 skateboarding	○	○
5 playing tennis	○	○

3 **Write. What are you good at or not very good at?**

👍 I'm good at _____

👎 I'm not very good at _____ yet.

4 💬 **Look at 3. Talk in pairs.**

I'm good at doing gymnastics. I'm not very good at playing baseball.

I'm good at playing baseball – I can teach you!

Talk buddies

I can talk about my abilities.

37

LESSON 4
Story

Eleni's gymnastics journal

1 Look. Which activities are in the story?

2 🎧 3.7 Listen and read. What is Eleni's specialty?

bars

beam

1 November 10th

I'm Eleni, I have lots of hobbies. I like playing badminton, roller skating, and trampolining. My favorite hobby is doing gymnastics – I love it. This is me. I'm doing a bar routine. I'm really good at bars – it's my specialty! I'm not very good at beam, so I don't like it much.

2 November 12th

I'm having a terrible day at the gym. I'm doing the beam very badly. I fall off a lot! I want to do my favorite things – not beam exercises!

3 November 17th

That's it! I'm stopping gymnastics! I quit! I fall off the beam all the time – seven times today. It hurts!

4 November 20th

I'm watching my brother, Alex. He's skateboarding really well. He's visually impaired, but he's very good at skateboarding. He doesn't have any problems balancing like me. I ask him how he does it … Alex says he uses his other senses to help him balance. I can try that on the beam!

Think!
Which senses do you think Eleni's brother uses to balance?
Go to to page 121 to find out!

38

5 November 22nd

I'm back at gymnastics again. I'm working really hard at beam. I'm thinking about my brother on his skateboard. I'm closing my eyes on the beam and using my other senses. It's not easy, but I'm enjoying it now.

6 November 27th

Look – that's me winning a gold medal at a gymnastics competition! No, it's not a medal for beam, it's a medal for bar … But I wasn't last in beam, I was fifth. I can do it!

3 Read again and write answers.

1. What are Eleni's hobbies?
   _____
2. What is Eleni's favorite hobby?
   _____
3. What is Alex good at?
   _____
4. What does Eleni win a medal for?
   _____

4 Think and answer.

1. Why does Eleni want to stop doing gymnastics?
2. Why does she decide to continue doing gymnastics?
3. Why does Eleni close her eyes? Does this help her try again?

5 Act out the story. Then reflect.

Reflect
You are not very good at an activity. How can you try again?

He's skateboarding really well. … I ask him how he does it …

I'm working really hard at beam. … I can do it!

Storytellers

I can read a story about self-motivation.

LESSON 5
Vocabulary and Grammar

1 🎧 3.8 **Listen and say. Then tell a friend.**

 1 quickly

 2 slowly

 3 carefully

 4 safely

 5 badly

6 well

Ways to learn
A word to describe a **thing** + **ly** = a word to describe an **action**.

Change the words so that they describe actions.

sad	quiet	slow
loud	brave	

2 🎧 3.9 **Listen, read, and write answers.**

Alex: Tell me what's happening in the baseball game, Carla. I can't see very well.

Carla: OK. Eleni is throwing the ball really carefully. Ezra is hitting the ball badly.

Alex: Oh, no. He usually plays well!

Carla: I know! Now it's Kai's turn to bat. Eleni is throwing the ball quickly … Wow! Kai hits the ball really well. It's going a long way. He's running very quickly. It's a home run! Kai and his team are celebrating loudly!

Alex: Yes, I can hear that very well!

1 Who is throwing the ball quickly?
___

2 Who is hitting the ball badly?
___

3 Who is hitting the ball well?
___

4 Who is celebrating loudly?
___

Grammar Heroes
She's playing badminton **well**.
They're snowboarding **safely**.
He's cheering **happily**.

3 💬 **Think of words to describe actions. Play *Opposites*.**

I do my homework slowly.

I roller skate quickly.

I can describe how people do actions.

40

LESSON 6
Listening and Speaking

1 ▶ Watch the video and match.

1. Riley is walking …   a) quietly.
2. Riley is skating …   b) quickly.
3. Riley is drinking … c) well.
4. Riley is sleeping … d) slowly.

2 🎧 Look at the game cards. Listen and write *K (Kai)* or *C (Carla)*.

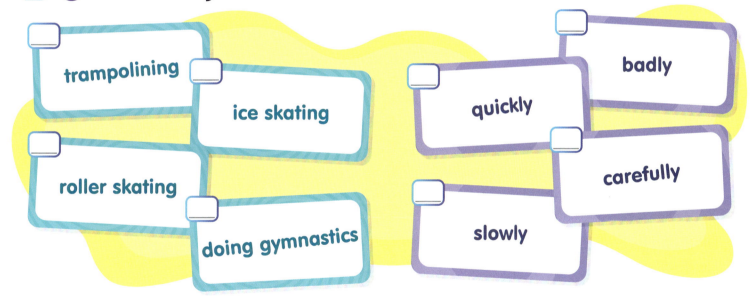

trampolining · ice skating · roller skating · doing gymnastics · quickly · badly · carefully · slowly

Let's communicate!

3 💬 Make activity and adverb cards. Then play *What am I doing?*

Go online Communication Kit

Are you playing baseball quickly?

Yes!

I can use game cards to talk about how we are doing actions.

41

LESSON 7
Myself and others

Motivating myself

1 Lessons 1 and 4 Think and write R (Riley) or E (Eleni).

Not good at yet
- a) beam ☐
- b) making friends ☐

Solution
- c) She talks to her mom and dad, then tries again for the team. ☐
- d) She watches her brother and tries again. ☐

2 3.11 Read, reflect, and share ideas. Then listen and choose.

I love skateboarding. I'm really good at it, too. All my friends enjoy roller skating. I'm not very good at roller skating. I don't like it, but I want to be with my friends.

What do you think Liam does?
- a) He doesn't practice roller skating.
- b) He practices roller skating, but stops because it's difficult.
- c) He practices roller skating a lot until he's good at it.

3 Read and check (✔). What can you say to help you try again?

1. I can learn and try again. ◯
2. I can work hard and do this. ◯
3. I can't do this. I want to stop. ◯
4. This is too hard. ◯

Useful Language
I'm not good at roller skating **yet**.
I want to learn.
I can get better!

4 Think and answer. Then share ideas.
- Which two things aren't you good at (yet)?
- What can you do to get better?

I can do this!

Be a hero!

Write a motto to help you try again.

42   **Self-awareness** I can recognize ways to motivate myself.

Blood and circulation

LESSON 8
Science — My world

1 ▶ Watch the video and check (✓).

Which parts of the body do you hear?
a) brain ○   b) face ○   c) heart ○

2 🎧 **Explore** Read, listen, and circle.

a) Blood takes **oxygen** / **blood vessels** around the body.
b) The heart pumps **quickly** / **slowly** when we are sleeping.

How does blood move around the body?

Blood moves around our bodies to take **oxygen** and food to all the different parts of the body. Our body needs oxygen and food to work and move, but how does the blood move around? The **heart** pumps the blood. It **pumps** the blood through **blood vessels**. Can you feel your heart pumping? Can you see the blood vessels on the back of your hand? In your body there are more than 95,000 kilometers of blood vessels!

When does the heart pump slowly and quickly?

When we are resting or sleeping, the heart pumps slowly. But the muscles in our body need more oxygen and food when we are moving. The heart pumps quickly when we are doing exercise. Think about when you play your favorite sport — can you feel your heart pumping quickly?

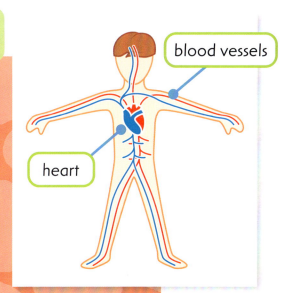

Did you know?
The heart pumps blood to every part of your body in only 60 seconds!

3 💡 **Think** Check (✓). Whose heart is pumping quickly?

Try it!
Measure your heart rate when resting and after a minute of jumping jacks. Why is there a difference?

I can read and understand about the heart and blood.

LESSON 9
Project

A sports journal

1 (Review) Look, read, and match. Then listen and check.

a. In this picture, I'm practicing hard. It isn't easy! I'm hitting the ball into the net a lot, but I'm enjoying it.

b. This is my first tennis competition. I'm hitting the ball really well! I'm good at it now.

c. This is my first tennis lesson with my teacher. I'm playing very badly, but I want to learn.

2 (Get ready) Think about your favorite sport. Imagine you are doing it now. Tell a friend.

- What is the sport?
- How are you doing it?
- Describe your actions.
- Are you good at it yet?

I'm skateboarding slowly and carefully. I'm not very good at it yet!

3 (Create) Make your sports journal.

Workbook page 37

 Writing: sports journal
- Link two sentences with different ideas using *but*.
- Put words like *badly*, *well*, and *beautifully* **after** the action word.

4 (Share) Present your sports journal.

Tips
Presentation
☐ Describe what is happening in the pictures.
☐ Describe how you are doing the action.
☐ Don't read from your project – look up at the class.

44   I can make and present a sports journal.

LESSON 10 Review

I can do it!

Movie challenge
How many ways can you describe Riley doing different things?

1 🎧 3.14 **Listen and circle.**

1. She's good at **ice hockey** / **skateboarding**. She's playing **carefully** / **safely**.
2. She isn't very good at **cycling** / **roller skating** yet.
3. He's playing **tennis** / **basketball**. He's hitting the ball **quietly** / **loudly**.
4. He's good at **gymnastics** / **trampolining**. He's jumping **slowly** / **well**.

2 💬 **Write descriptions of the pictures. Then share your answers.**

He's ice skating _____ .
He's very _____ ice skating.

_____
_____

> He's ice skating well.   He's ice skating beautifully.

I can ...

- 💬 describe people playing sports ○
- 📖 read a story ○
- 🎨 make and present a sports journal ○
- 🙆 try again at things I'm not very good at ○

Sticker time

☑ **I completed Unit 3!**

Extra Lesson

Go online
Big Project

45

4 Amazing animals

What animal words do you know? Share ideas.

hippo

Video story

1 🎬 4A Watch the video. Check (✓). Which animals does Judy help?

1 2 3 4

2 🎬 4A Watch again and answer.

1. How is Judy different from the other police officers?
2. Why doesn't Chief Bogo give Judy a dangerous job?
3. Why don't the elephants give Nick an ice cream?

LESSON 1 Vocabulary

3 🎧 Listen, find, and say. Then tell a friend.

1   2   3   4

4 🎵 Listen, chant, and act.

> Animals are all different,
> They're amazing, too!
> A cheetah is quiet and quick,
> A hippo is very big!
> An otter is furry and long,
> A buffalo is very strong!
> A rabbit is cute and small,
> And it isn't very tall!
> So animals are all different,
> And we're all different, too!

5 💬 Act out and play *Guess my animal*. **Talk buddies**

> You're big and strong. You have horns … Are you a buffalo?

> Yes, I am!

otter

cheetah

buffalo

I can name animals.

LESSON 2
Vocabulary

1 🎧 4.3 **Listen and say. Then tell a friend.**

1 cute

2 hairy

3 large

4 friendly

5 tiny

6 fierce

7 smart

8 furry

2 🎧 4.4 **Listen and say describing words.**

3 **Look, read, and match.**

1. It's cute and furry. It isn't tiny, but it isn't large.
2. It's really smart. It can be friendly and fierce! It isn't hairy.
3. It's fierce and large. It isn't friendly and it isn't furry.
4. It's large and hairy. It's friendly!

Guess what?
Hippos are large, but they can run fast. They can be fierce and dangerous, too!

a

b

c

d

4 **Write three riddles for animals in 1. Then play *What is it?***

It's tiny and hairy.
It's not very smart.

It's tiny and hairy.
It's not very smart.

Picture 2!

Talk buddies

I can describe animals.

48

LESSON 3
Grammar

1 🎧 4.5 **Listen, read, and match.**

1. He's furrier than Judy. Judy is smarter than him. He's happier than Chief Bogo.

2. He's larger than Judy and he's stronger. Judy is friendlier than him.

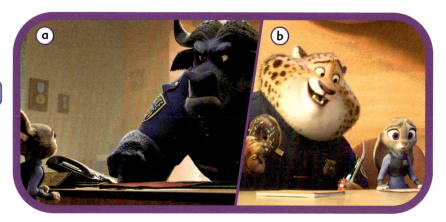

2 🎧 4.6 **Listen and write A (Alex) or C (Carla).**

> **Grammar Heroes**
> A rabbit is **cuter than** a snake.
> A buffalo is **hairier than** a frog.
> A hippo is **bigger than** an otter.
> good ➜ better   bad ➜ worse

3 **Look at 2 and write.**

> faster than   fiercer than
> hairier than   smaller than

1. The otter is _____ the cheetah.
2. The fox is _____ the rabbit.
3. The buffalo is _____ the hippo.
4. The cheetah is _____ all other animals!

4 💬 **Think of an animal. Then play *Guess the animal*.**

Is it smaller and cuter than a fox?

Yes, it is.

Is it a mouse?

Yes!

I can compare animals.

49

LESSON 4
Story

THE ZOO

1 Look. What animals can you see?

2 🎧 4.7 Listen and read. Which is the new animal at the zoo?

① Our mom is a vet. We go with her to the zoo. Mom asks the zookeeper, Jeff, "Can I see the polar bear?" Jeff says, "No, it's sick. I'm waiting for the vet." He doesn't think mom is a zoo vet because she's a tiny woman!

② We sit down and wait for mom.
"You can't sit there," says Jeff, grumpily.
"Can we come around the zoo with you?" I ask.
"OK," says Jeff, but he isn't very happy about it.
We help Jeff feed the hippos and the buffalos.
"There's a new animal in the rainforest biome," says Jeff. We look up into the trees. Eleni sees it.
"It's a sloth!" she says. "It's the slowest animal in the world," I say. "You're smart!" says Jeff.

③ Just then, I hear crying. I look around and see a little boy. I run over. "Do you need help?" I ask. "Yes! I'm lost!" says the boy. I tell Jeff and we help the little boy find his parents. "You are nice and friendly kids," says Jeff.

Think!
Which is the hippo's food?
Go to to page 122 to find out!

50

④ Jeff takes us to his office and gives us hot chocolate to thank us. Then he looks at his calendar and looks grumpy again. "What's wrong?" I ask. "Next week Park School is coming for a visit. That school is in a really bad neighborhood, and the kids are the worst. They aren't friendly or smart like you."

⑤ "Jeff!" I say, "We go to Park School and so do our friends. They are smart and friendly kids!" "Oh," says Jeff, with a red face, "I'm sorry – I guess I was wrong about that."

3 Read again and write answers.

1. Which animals do the children feed?
   _____
2. Where does the sloth live?
   _____
3. Why is the little boy sad?
   _____
4. Why does Jeff give Eleni and Alex hot chocolate?
   _____

4 Think and answer.

1. Why doesn't Jeff think Mom is a vet?
2. Do you think Jeff likes Alex and Eleni at the start of the story?
3. Why does Jeff think children from Park School are not friendly or smart?
4. Is he right about the children from Park School? Why/Why not?

5 💬 Act out the story. Then reflect.

Storytellers

Reflect
How can you help people not to make stereotypes?

... the kids are the worst. They aren't friendly or smart like you.

We go to Park School and so do our friends.

I can read a story about challenging stereotypes.

LESSON 5
Vocabulary and Grammar

1 🎧 4.8 **Listen and say. Then tell a friend.**

1 sloth

2 shrew

3 wolf

4 panda

5 polar bear

6 yak

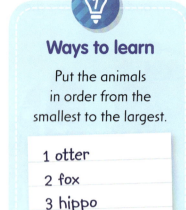

Ways to learn

Put the animals in order from the smallest to the largest.

1 otter
2 fox
3 hippo

2 🎧 4.9 **Listen, read, and number in order.**

Carla: That's Judy. She's the cutest, smartest police officer in Zootopia. I don't think rabbits are smart in real life!
Ezra: Is that cheetah a police officer, too?
Carla: Yes, that's Clawhauser. Cheetahs are the fastest animals in the world!
Ezra: Is he fast in the movie?
Carla: No, he isn't.
Ezra: Is that a shrew?
Carla: Yes, that's Mr. Big. But he's the tiniest character in the movie.
Ezra: Who's that?
Carla: That's Yax the Yak. He's the hairiest character. In real life, Yaks have long hair because they live in cold places.

a
b
c
d

Grammar Heroes

I think wolves are **the fiercest** animals.
Blue whales are **the largest** animals on Earth.
the best   **the worst**

3 💬 **Think of animals. Then play *Sentence trio*.**

A sloth is furry.
A panda is furrier.
A polar bear is the furriest.

Talk buddies

Go online
Phonics

52   I can describe animals.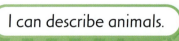

LESSON 6
Listening and Speaking

1 ▶ Watch the video and circle.

① The thief is **smaller** / **larger** than Judy.

② Judy is the **tiniest** / **biggest** animal in Little Rodentia.

③ Judy is the **fiercest** / **friendliest** police officer in Zootopia.

2 🎧 Listen and check (✓) the winning game card.

Let's communicate!

3 💬 Make animal cards and play.

Go online — Communication Kit

Fast! Which animal is the fastest?

My animal has 75 points.

The cheetah is the fastest. 100 points for "fast." I win!

I can use animal cards to make comparisons.

LESSON 7
Myself and others

Recognizing stereotypes

1    **Think and match.**

a) They are the worst children.

b) He is fiercer than other animals.

c) The other police officers are better and braver than her.

d) She can't be a vet because she is tiny.

2 **Look, think, and write one word for each person.**

| architect | cute | doctor | friendly | fun | hospital cleaner | nurse | smart | teacher |

_____   _____   _____   _____

3 🎧 💬 **Listen. What do more than half of the class write? Then share ideas.**

Useful Language
Most people think that …
Why do you think that?
I think that, too.

4 💬 **What can you say to people who think these things?**

Short people aren't good at sports.

Girls are smarter than boys.

Old people are boring.

Be a hero!
How can you remember **not** to stereotype? Write a message to yourself.

54 **Responsible decision-making** I can recognize stereotypes.

Biomes

LESSON 8
Science
My world

1   Watch the video and circle.

Which biome is in the picture?   tundra / **rainforest**

2 **Explore** Read, listen, and circle.

Biomes

a **Pandas** / **Rabbits** here have larger ears to keep cool.
b **Tundra** / **Rainforest** is the coldest biome.

Desert **biomes** have the hottest, driest **climate**. Not many plants grow because the ground is sand and rocks. Rabbit **species** here have larger ears to help keep them cool.

Aquatic means water. Aquatic biomes are oceans, lakes, and rivers. Most aquatic animals are not furry and they use their tails to swim. The largest species of animals, the blue whale, lives in an aquatic biome.

There are two types of forest biome: hot, wet forests are called **rainforests**. Other forest biomes are colder. A lot of forest animals are good at climbing, like sloths and pandas. They climb because it is safer to live in the trees, and they eat leaves.

Tundra biomes are the coldest. Snow and ice cover the ground for much of the year. The animal species that live here are the furriest. They are often white to hide in the snow.

Grassland biomes have a warm or hot climate, but they are rainier than desert biomes. There is lots of grass and there are fast animals here.

Try it!
Look at a map. What different biomes are there in your country? Which animals live there?

3   **Think** Complete the table.

climbs trees to keep safe   ~~large ears to keep cool~~   white fur to hide in the snow   uses its tail to swim

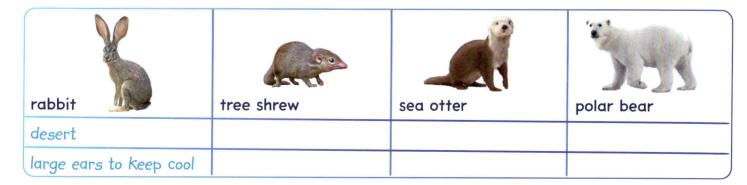

rabbit	tree shrew	sea otter	polar bear
desert			
large ears to keep cool			

I can read and understand about biomes.

LESSON 9 Project

An animal display

1 (Review) **Listen and write.** desert fastest forests tiniest tundra

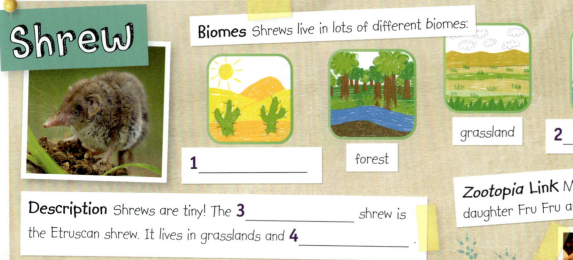

Shrew

Biomes Shrews live in lots of different biomes:

1 _____   forest   grassland   2 _____

Description Shrews are tiny! The **3** _____ shrew is the Etruscan shrew. It lives in grasslands and **4** _____.

Zootopia Link Mr. Big and his daughter Fru Fru are shrews.

Amazing fact! Shrews have the **5** _____ heartbeat of all animals. Their heart beats 800 times per minute.

2 (Get ready) **Choose an animal to research. Tell a friend what you know about:**

Where it lives — What it looks like — Any interesting facts

Tips
Self-management
- ☐ Choose interesting facts.
- ☐ Organize the information into subject areas
- ☐ When you make notes, don't make full sentences.

3 (Create) **Make notes and create an animal display.** Workbook page 49

4 (Share) **Share your animal display with the class.**

Writing: An animal display
- Write sub-headings for each subject area.
- Use scientific words about biomes and species.

56   I can create an animal display.

I can do it!

LESSON 10 Review

1 🎧 4.14 **Listen and write. Then match.**

1. This is Chief Bogo. He's a _____ . He isn't the _____ character in Zootopia.

2. This is Flash. He's a _____ . He's the _____ character in Zootopia.

3. This is Yax. He's a _____ . He's the _____ character in Zootopia.

a
b
c

2 **Write about Judy.**

This is Judy. She's a 1_____ . She is the 2_____ police officer in Zootopia. She isn't the 3_____ character in Zootopia.

3 💬 **Play** *Describe the animal.*

sloth — A sloth is slower than an otter

polar bear — A polar bear is furrier than a hippo.

Movie challenge

How many animals from *Zootopia* can you say in 30 seconds? Go!

I can ...
- name and identify animals ☐
- read a story ☐
- make an animal display ☐
- recognize stereotypes ☐

Sticker time

✓ I completed Unit 4!

Extra Lesson Go online Big Project

57

LESSON 1 **Vocabulary**

3 🎧 Listen, find, and say. Then tell a friend.

4 🎵 Listen, chant, and act.

A long time ago in London town,
People traveled by ship.
They lived in houses,
They cooked on the fire,
And they danced, danced, danced!

A long time ago in America,
The Powhatan people traveled by boat.
They lived in huts,
They cooked on the fire,
And they danced, danced, danced!

5 💬 How is Pocahontas' life different from yours? Share ideas.

Pocahontas lives in a hut, but I live in an apartment.

Pocahontas wears a skirt, but I wear pants.

Talk buddies

carriage

ship

port

I can name things from the past.

59

LESSON 2
Vocabulary

1 🎧 5.3 **Listen and say. Then tell a friend.**

 1 farm
 2 hunt
 3 carry
 4 travel

 5 sail
 6 visit
 7 pick
 8 use

2 🎧 5.4 💬 **Listen and say. Then play *Word chain*.**

3 **Read and match. Then write.**

1. In the past, people traveled in carriages and on horseback.
2. In the past, people farmed by hand.
3. In the past, the Powhatan people lived in huts.

a. Today, people _____ with machines.
b. Today, Powhatan people _____ in houses and apartments.
c. Today, people _____ in cars and on buses.

? Guess what?
Pocahontas was a real person! She was born around 1595. Her father was the Powhatan chief.

4 💬 **Write sentences using the actions in 1. Then play *Guess the action*.**

I hunt animals.

Are you hunting?

Yes, I am.

 Talk buddies

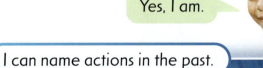
I can name actions in the past.

60

LESSON 3
Grammar

1 🎧 5.5 **Listen, read, and match.**

1. He traveled by ship. He didn't farm. He lived in a house.
2. They didn't live in houses. They lived in huts. They didn't travel by horse and carriage.

2 🎧 5.6 **Listen and put a ✓ or ✗.**

In the movie the boy …
1. lived in a city.
2. lived on a farm.
3. picked fruit.
4. farmed animals.
5. wanted to stay on the farm.

Grammar Heroes
She **carries** fruit. ➜ She **carried** fruit.
We **don't farm** ➜ We **didn't farm**.

3 **Look at 2 and write sentences.**

- live / city — He didn't live in a city.
- live / farm — ___
- pick / fruit — ___
- farm / animals — ___
- want / stay / farm — ___

4 💬 **Write about a character from a movie. Then play *Guess who?*** Talk buddies

Her family farmed carrots. She didn't hunt animals. She worked as a police officer.

Is she Judy from *Zootopia*?

I can understand and talk about the past.

LESSON 4 Story

Grandma's story

1 Look. Who's telling the story?

2 🎧 5.7 Listen and read. What was Grandma Dana's job?

① Ezra and Carla are talking to Ezra's grandma in London. "Hi Grandma Dana! Carla and I are doing a project about life in the past." "Am I from the past? I am very old!" says Grandma Dana. "Not that old!" laughs Ezra.
"Let me tell you all about my past …"

② "I was born in Jamaica. I lived on a farm. I helped on the farm and picked fruit. Then I studied to be a nurse. There was more work for nurses in London, so I traveled there. I sailed across the ocean on a ship with lots of other people from the Caribbean.

I was very excited. I worked in a hospital in London. There were lots of friendly people, but some people didn't like us. They didn't like us because we looked different, we cooked different food, and we enjoyed different music. Some people didn't want Caribbean people to live in their houses."

③ "That's terrible!" says Ezra, "Where did you live?"

"I lived in a room in a friend's house. Your grandpa stayed in a room in the same house. We married a few years later and moved into our own house. We worked hard, but we were very happy!"

Think!
Which is the festival in London Grandma Dana talks about?
Go to to page 123 to find out!

④ "Is life better in London now?" asks Carla.

"Yes, its very different. People love our traditional food and music now! There is a big festival and parade to celebrate Caribbean culture in London every year. People from different cultures all celebrate together."

"I want to go to the festival!" says Carla. Grandma Dana walks away.

⑤ "Where's Grandma?" asks Ezra.

"Look!" laughs Carla, "She's in her colorful festival dress!"

"What are you waiting for?" asks Grandma Dana, "Let's dance!"

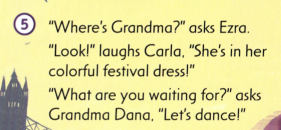

3 Read again and complete.

1. Grandma Dana _____ fruit on a farm.
2. She _____ to be a nurse in Jamaica.
3. She _____ to London by ship.
4. She _____ in a hospital in London.

4 Think and answer.

1. How did Grandma Dana feel when she arrived in London?
2. Why didn't some people like people from the Caribbean?
3. How are things different in London now?

5 Act out the story. Then reflect.

Reflect
How do you celebrate other cultures?

People love our traditional food and music now!

There is a big festival and parade to celebrate Caribbean culture …

Storytellers

I can read a story about celebrating different cultures.

LESSON 5
Vocabulary and Grammar

1 🎧 5.8 **Listen and say. Then tell a friend.**

1 pyramid

2 corn

3 basket

4 oven

5 spear

6 bow and arrow

Ways to learn

Draw a picture for each word!

pyramid

2 🎧 5.9 **Listen, read, and write.**

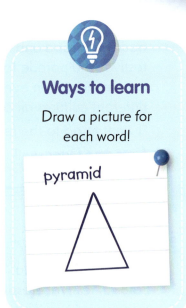

Kai: Which ancient culture did you study, Carla?
Carla: I studied the Ancient Egyptians.
Kai: Did Egyptians live in 1_____?
Carla: No, they didn't. They lived in houses.
Kai: Did Egyptians farm 2_____?
Carla: No, they didn't. They farmed other cereals, vegetables, and fruit.
Kai: Did they hunt animals?
Carla: Yes, they did. They hunted with 3_____, and bows and 4_____.

Kai: Did they cook in 5_____?
Carla: Yes, they did. They cooked on wood fire ovens.
Kai: Did they use baskets?
Carla: Yes, they did. They used baskets to carry fruit and vegetables.

Grammar Heroes
Did they **live** in huts?
No, they **didn't**.
Did they **use** baskets?
Yes, they **did**.

3 💬 **Play** *Three in a row.*

Did you hunt animals yesterday? — No, I didn't.
Did you cook yesterday? — Yes, I did.

Talk buddies

I can ask and answer about things in the past.

Extra Lesson

Go online
Phonics

LESSON 6
Listening and Speaking

1 🔊 Watch the video and write answers.

1. Did the women pick corn and fruit?
   _____
2. Did Pocahontas carry the fruit?
   _____
3. Did the Powhatan people live in pyramids?
   _____

2 🎧 Listen and read the questionnaire. Put a ✔ or ✘.

Ancient Greeks

	Girls	Boys
1 learned to read and write	○	○
2 learned to make baskets and cook	○	○
3 worked as farmers, fishermen, or craftsmen	○	○
4 learned to hunt	○	○
5 cooked with ovens	○	○

Let's communicate!

Did Powhatan women work?

3 💬 Use the questionnaire. Ask, answer, and check (✔).

Go online — Communication Kit

Yes, they did.

I can use a questionnaire to ask and answer about ancient cultures.

65

LESSON 7
Myself and others

celebrating our cultures

1 Lessons 1 and 4 5A **Think and match.**

a) I want to understand my friend's culture. ☐

b) We have fun learning about a different culture. ☐

2 **Look and reflect. Then share ideas.**

1. What is the problem with the class?
2. What can the children do to celebrate other groups?
3. What can the teacher do to help?

3 5.11 **Listen, read, and number. Which monster has the best attitude?**

a) I don't want to learn about the culture and celebrations of the other monsters. It's boring. ☐

b) I want to learn all about the other cultures. Their celebrations are fun – we can celebrate together. It's cool to be different! ☐

c) It's OK to learn about other cultures, but my culture is the best. I'm very proud of my culture – the others aren't interesting. ☐

4 **Write answers. Then share ideas.**

- What different cultures are in your town or city?
- What do you like from those different cultures?

Useful Language
I think your culture is interesting.
That sounds fun!

Be a hero!

Bring in an object or picture that shows your culture. Tell your friends about it.

Social awareness I can learn to celebrate other cultures and diversity.

Ships and forces

LESSON 8
My world

1 Watch the video and answer.

How did people travel across oceans?

2 **Explore** Read, listen, and circle.

a. The two types of forces are **push** / **sink** and pull.
b. The wind **pulls** / **pushes** a ship's sails.
c. When a ship stays on the water, it's **sinking** / **floating**.
d. **An anchor** / **Sails** stop(s) a ship.

Forces

How do things move? A **force** moves objects. There are two types of forces — a **push** and a **pull**. Ships and boats use force to move and to **float** on the water.

Floating and sinking

When a ship is in water, there are two forces which act on it. One force is the water pushing up. The other force is the ship's weight — how heavy it is — pushing down. It's the same for all objects. When the weight of an object pushing down is the same or less than the push up of the water, it floats. "Floats" means it stays on the water. When the weight of an object pushing down is more than the push up of the water, it **sinks**. "Sinks" means it goes under the water.

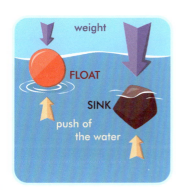

Moving

Forces move objects that can't move by themselves. The force from the wind pushes the **sails** of a ship. This moves it across the ocean.

Ships use **anchors** to stop. An anchor is heavy. The anchor sinks to the bottom of the ocean and pulls the ship to a stop.

3 **Think** Read again and write.

apple   eraser   feather   pencil   ruler   shell

Float: _____ , _____ , _____ , _____

Sink: _____ , _____

Try it!
Find out if the objects float or sink. Were you right?

I can read and understand about ships and forces.

67

LESSON 9 Project

A class culture book

1   (Review) Listen, read, and write.

Our Culture: Polish

Some people from Poland **1**_____ here by ship 100 years ago. In Poland, many families **2**_____ on farms. They **3**_____ potatoes and apples. They **4**_____ animals.

2 (Get ready) In groups, decide on a culture and find out about it.

Did they sail?

Did they farm?

Did they hunt animals?

Did they live in huts?

Tips
Collaboration
- ☐ Make decisions together.
- ☐ Listen and give others time to speak.
- ☐ Give different people in the group different tasks.

3 (Create) Listen to your friends' ideas and create your group page of the class culture book.

 Writing: class culture book
- Write a first draft of your sentences.
- Check your first drafts together.
- Write a final draft to go in the class book.

Workbook page 61

4 (Share) Put the class culture book together and share your page with the class.

I can find out about different cultures and make a class culture book.

LESSON 10 Review

I can do it!

1 Look and write sentences.

1. They / travel <u>They traveled by horse and carriage.</u>
2. They / carry _____
3. They / cook _____
4. They / live _____

2 💬 What didn't they do? Look at 1 and share ideas.

> They didn't travel by car.

> They didn't live in huts.

Movie challenge
Say all the things the Powhatan people did and didn't do in 30 seconds. Go!

3 🎧 5.14 Listen, read, and write answers.

1. Did Ezra enjoy the ancestry project? <u>Yes, he did.</u>
2. Did he learn about Ancient Egypt? _____
3. Did they make arrows and spears in Ancient Ghana?
   _____
4. Did they use horses to carry things across the desert?
   _____

I can ...

- 💬 name past actions and objects ☐
- 📖 read a story ☐
- 🎨 make a culture class book ☐
- 👥 celebrate diversity in my class ☐

Sticker time

✓ I completed Unit 5!

Test your progress with English Benchmark Young Learners

 Extra Lesson

 Go online Big Project

69

6 Adventure time

do archery

What was your last adventure? Share ideas.

Video story

eat outdoors

1 Watch the video. Check (✓). Who did Merida catch fish with?

1 2 3 4

2 Watch again and answer.

1. Why was Merida's mom angry?
2. What did Merida teach her bear mom?
3. How did they start to build their relationship?

LESSON 1 **Vocabulary**

3 🎧 Listen, find, and say. Then tell a friend.
6.1

1 2 3 4

4 🎵 Listen, chant, and act.
6.2

> Let's go on an adventure!
> There are lots of things to do,
> We can go fishing and catch a fish or two!
>
> Let's go on an adventure!
> There are lots of things to do,
> We can go rock climbing and eat outdoors, too!
>
> Let's go on an adventure!
> There are lots of things to do,
> We can do archery and shoot an arrow or two!

5 💬 Act out and play *Guess the action*.   **Talk buddies**

Are you doing archery?   Yes, I am.

go rock climbing

catch fish

I can name outdoor activities.

71

LESSON 2
Vocabulary

1 🎧 **Listen and say. Then tell a friend.**

 1 swim outdoors
 2 go on an adventure
 3 build a den
 4 get lost

 5 make a campfire
 6 see wild animals
 7 go mountain biking
 8 go rafting

2 🎧 **Listen and say the activity.**

3 **Look, read, and match. Then complete with words from 1.**

1 I'm outside. I'm cold and I want to cook some fish. What can I do?

2 I'm in the river. Brrrr! It's very cold!

3 I think this is the wrong path. Oh, no! I don't know where we are.

Guess what?
Lots of wild animals live in cities!

a    b    c

_____   _____   _____

4 💬 **Write and rank the activities in 1. Then share ideas.**

1 I love 😀
4 I like 🙂
8 I don't like ☹️

I don't like getting lost.

I love going rafting.

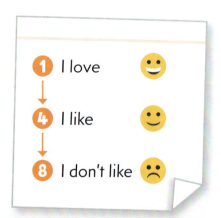

Talk buddies

I can name outdoor activities.

LESSON 3
Grammar

1 🎧 6.5 **Listen, read, and check (✓).**

1. Merida caught a fish.
2. Merida didn't catch a fish.

2 🎧 6.6 **Listen and check (✓). What did Eleni and Ezra do in the video game?**

Grammar Heroes
I **went** mountain biking. → I **didn't go** mountain biking.
She **got** lost in the forest. → She **didn't get** lost in the forest.

	Ezra	Eleni
build a den		
get lost		
go rafting		
make a campfire		
catch a fish		
see wild animals		

3 **Look at 2. Write sentences for Ezra and Eleni.**

Ezra ➕ _He built a den._   ➖ _He didn't go rafting._
      ➕ He _____.   ➖ He _____.

Eleni ➕ She _____.   ➖ She _____.
      ➕ She _____.   ➖ She _____.

4 💬 **Think of outdoor activities. Then play *Sentence chain*.**

I went on an adventure.

I didn't go on an adventure. I did archery.

Talk buddies

I can talk about activities in the past with irregular verbs.

73

LESSON 4
Story

Ezra's Camp Blog

Home
About
Follow

1. Look. Where are the children?

2. 🎧 6.7 Listen and read. What did Ezra and his friends do at camp?

What I learned last weekend.

① I went to an Adventure Camp with my friends last weekend.

We were very excited.

On the first day, we went mountain biking in the forest. The plan was to go to a lake to swim outdoors and see the sunset.

② I was in a group with my friend, Kai, for mountain biking. We didn't have cell phones, but Kai had a camera. He loves taking pictures.

We saw lots of wild animals!

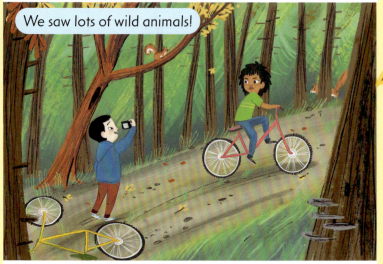

Kai took pictures of all the birds and wild animals he saw. I wanted to go faster and get to the lake. I was angry with Kai because we were far away from the rest of the group. "Come on, Kai!" I yelled. "Be quiet, Ezra!" he yelled back, "You're scaring the wild animals!" We argued a lot.

③

Soon, we were lost.

We looked up and there were lots of different paths. We saw the sunset and it started to get dark. We were lost in the dark! This was because of Kai. I was so angry with him.

Think! Which picture didn't Kai take?

Go to to page 124 to find out!

74

4 Then Kai said. "I have an idea!". "What?" I said. "Look at this picture I took – it's that tree there!" "Oh, yes!" We followed the path to the tree and looked at the next picture. We had fun finding all the things in the pictures and we found our way back to camp.

"Good job, Kai!" I said, "I'm sorry I got angry."

"I'm sorry I got angry, too," said Kai, "And I'm sorry you didn't swim outdoors." "That's OK," I said, "We had a better adventure!"

3 Read again and write answers.

1. Who wrote the blog?
   _____
2. What did Ezra want to do?
   _____
3. What did Kai take pictures of?
   _____
4. How did they find their way back to camp?
   _____

4 Think and answer.

1. Were Ezra and Kai friends before they went mountain biking?
2. Why did Ezra get angry with Kai?
3. How did Ezra and Kai build their relationship again?

5 Act out the story. Then reflect.

Reflect
You argue with a friend. What can you do?

Good job, Kai! … I'm sorry I got angry.

That's OK … We had a better adventure!

I can read a story about building a relationship.

75

LESSON 5
Vocabulary and Grammar

1 🎧 6.8 **Listen and say. Then tell a friend.**

1 find fossils

2 go stargazing

3 catch a leaf

4 throw stones in a stream

5 explore a cave

6 see the sunset / sunrise

Ways to learn
Make a verbs list.

catch → caught
find → found
go → went
say → said
teach → taught
throw → threw

2 🎧 6.9 **Listen, read, and write.**

On Friday …

Kai: What do you want to do this weekend?

Eleni: I want to 1_____ a leaf, find a fossil, go stargazing, and 2_____ stones in a stream.

Kai: Sounds awesome!

On Monday …

Kai: How was your weekend? What did you do?

Eleni: Well, we 3_____ mountain biking. I found a stream and I 4_____ stones in.

Kai: You did some fun things!

Eleni: Yes, but I didn't 5_____ any fossils. I 6_____ a leaf!

Kai: Did it fall from a tree?

Eleni: No, my brother 7_____ it at me! We didn't go stargazing because it was late.

Grammar Heroes
What **did** she **do**?
She **went** mountain biking.
She **didn't find** a fossil.

3 💬 **Think about your last trip to the countryside. Ask and answer.**

What did you do in the countryside?

I explored a cave.

Talk buddies

I can ask and answer about activities in the past.

LESSON 6
Listening and Speaking

1 ▶ Watch the video and write answers.

1. Where did Merida and her mom go?
   _____
2. What did the bear mom eat?
   _____
3. Did they sleep in the cave?
   _____
4. When did Merida's mom change?
   _____

2 🎧 6.10 Listen, read, and check (✔). What did Carla do at Forest School?

Outdoor Activity List

1. find fossils ⭕
2. see the sunset ⭕
3. explore a cave ⭕
4. throw stones in a stream ⭕
5. make a fire ⭕
6. catch a fish ⭕
7. build a den ⭕
8. eat outdoors ⭕

Let's communicate!

3 💬 Write six things you did on an adventure. Then ask and answer.

Go online
Communication Kit

What did you do?

I went mountain biking

Did you throw stones in a stream?

No, I didn't.

I can use a list to talk about outdoor activities in the past.

77

LESSON 7
Myself and others

Building relationships

1 `Lessons 1 and 4` 🎬 💡 **Think and match. How did they build their relationship?**

a) They helped each other. ☐

b) They learned from each other. ☐

c) They had fun. ☐

2 💡 **What's important for building a relationship? Number in order.**

a) Help each other ☐   b) Say sorry ☐   c) Have fun together ☐

d) Learn from each other ☐   e) Listen to each other ☐

3 💬 🎧 **What can Adriana do? Read and share ideas. Then listen. Are your ideas the same as Karl's?**

Adriana

> Hi, Karl. I argued with my friend, Lucy, yesterday. I wanted her help, but she didn't listen to me. She knows I always want help with math, but she went out and had fun with our other friends. I had to do my homework by myself and I'm not very good at it.

4 💬 **Act out the conversation between Adriana and Lucy.**

Useful Language
I'm sorry we argued.
I'm sorry I didn't listen.
Let's talk about it.

I'm sorry I didn't help you, but I always do your math for you.

It's OK. I'm sorry I got angry and didn't listen to you.

Lucy

Adriana

Be a hero!
When you argue with someone, talk, listen, and say sorry.

Relationship skills I can learn to build relationships.

Living and non-living things

LESSON 8 — Science: My world

1 ▶ **Watch the video and answer.**

What living and non-living things are in your classroom?

2 🎧 **Explore** Read, listen, and circle.

a. People and **birds / trees** grow slowly.
b. Plants drink water through their **nutrients / roots**.
c. Eggs have growing **babies / seeds** inside them.

Living things Living things look very different from each other. People look different from trees. Fish look different from elephants. But all living things have some similarities.

Grow All living things grow. It is many years before some things become adults - like trees and people. Other things grow into adults in just a few months, for example, birds and flowering plants.

Eat and drink All animals eat food and drink water. Plants drink water through their roots. They make their own food from the sun! Living things need nutrients from food to make energy. They need energy to move and grow.

Breathe air Breathing in and out is something we do almost every second. Plants and animals use air to make energy. Animals use oxygen from the air with nutrients from food, to make energy.

Move Birds fly, monkeys climb, fish swim, and you run around. Animals move a lot! You don't see plants running around or flying, but plants can move very slowly. They move towards the sun to get more sunlight.

Reproduce To reproduce means to make new living things. Animals have babies or lay eggs with babies growing inside. Many plants make seeds that grow into more plants.

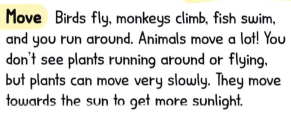

3 💡 **Think** Complete and add more words.

Living things	Non-living things
_____	_____
_____	_____

Try it!
Put a plant in sunlight. Watch it grow towards the sun.

cat   feather   rock   tree

I can read and understand about living and non-living things.

79

LESSON 9
Project

An outdoors scrapbook

1 (Review) **Listen, read, and write.**

> ate   caught   didn't go   fossil   made   ~~mountain biking~~   raft

A day outdoors!
I went **1** <u>mountain biking</u> in the forest with my mom, dad, and sister! We built a **2** _____ , but we **3** _____ rafting in the stream because it was a small raft. My sister's teddy bear went rafting!

My favorite things in the forest
- I **4** _____ a leaf!
- We **5** _____ a fire.
- We **6** _____ outdoors.
- I found a **7** _____ !

2 (Get ready) **Think about your outdoor adventures. Tell a friend about:**

places you went
activities you did
things you saw or found

> I went to the lake. I swam outdoors and explored a cave!

> Did you throw stones in the lake?

✏️ Writing: scrapbook
- Start sentences with a capital letter.
- Connect two ideas in a sentence with *and*, *but*, or *because*.
- Use bullet points (•) to make lists.

3 (Create) **Create your outdoors scrapbook and plan your presentation.**

Workbook page 73

4 (Share) **Present your scrapbook.**

Tips
Presentation
☐ Start your presentation with "Hello, I'd like to tell you about …"
☐ Don't read from your scrapbook.
☐ Let your friends ask questions.

I can make and present an outdoors scrapbook.

LESSON 10
Review

I can do it!

1 Read the postcard. Then look and put a ✓ or ✗.

Hi Grandpa,

I'm having an amazing time at adventure camp.

On the first day, we built a den in the forest. We saw lots of wild animals. Yesterday, I did archery. Some groups swam in the lake, but I didn't. I didn't go rafting either — I really wanted to! On the last night, we went stargazing.

See you soon,

Sol

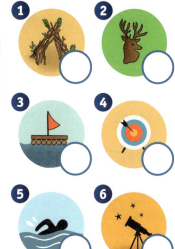

2 Imagine you went to an adventure camp. Complete the postcard for you.

Hi Grandma,

I'm having a _____ at adventure camp.
On the first day, I _____ and yesterday, I _____ . I didn't _____ , but I wanted to!
On the last night, we _____ .
See you soon, _____

Movie challenge

How many activities in the movie can you say in 30 seconds? Go!

Sticker time

I can ...

- 💬 talk about outdoor activities in the past
- 📖 read a story
- 🎨 make and present an outdoors scrapbook
- 🌍 build relationships

✓ I completed Unit 6!

81

7 Beach vacation

What can you find at the beach? Share ideas.

palm trees

Video story

1 Watch the video. Check (✓). Where does Moana want to go?

1   2   3

2 Watch again and answer.

1. What does Moana want to do?
2. Why does Moana's dad say, "Stay on the island!"?
3. What helps Moana to understand her dad's feelings?

LESSON 1 **Vocabulary**

3 🎧 **Listen, find, and say. Then tell a friend.**
7.1

1 2 3 4

coconuts

4 🎵 **Listen, chant, and act.**
7.2

We're going to go on an island vacation!
We're going to see palm trees on the beach.
We're going to eat coconuts,
We're going to have one each!

We're going to go on an island vacation!
We're going to explore some caves.
We're going to swim near the coral reef.
We're going to surf the waves!

5 💬 **Play *Guess the picture*.**

It's an island with mountains and palm trees.

That one!

Talk buddies

island

coral reef

I can name things on an island.

83

LESSON 2
Vocabulary

1 🎧 7.3 **Listen and say. Then tell a friend.**

1. walk on the sand

2. pack a suitcase

3. catch a plane

4. go to the swimming pool

5. paddle in the ocean

6. stay in a hotel

7. put on sunscreen

8. go snorkeling

2 🎧 7.4 💬 **Listen and say. Then play *Word chain*.**

3 **Look, read, and match. Then write.**

1. I'm under the water. I'm wearing a mask. I can see the coral reef.
2. My feet and legs are wet, but my body is dry. I'm jumping in the waves!
3. I'm sleeping in a big building near the beach. Our room has two beds.
4. On the beach, we need to do this every two hours. Careful, Dad, it's cold!

Guess what?
There are more than 20,000 islands in the southern Pacific Ocean.

a

b
go snorkeling

c

d

_____   _____   _____   _____

4 💬 **Write a riddle. Then play *Guess the beach activity*.**

I'm putting my clothes in a big bag.

I'm putting my clothes in a big bag.

Are you packing a suitcase?

Talk buddies

I can name beach vacation activities.

84

LESSON 3
Grammar

1 🎧 7.5 **Listen, read, and match.**

1. Moana is going to swim to her boat.
2. Moana is going to climb to the top of the mountain.

2 🎧 7.6 **Listen and check (✔). What are Eleni and Alex going to do?**

Grammar Heroes
I'm going to go on vacation this summer.
We**'re going to make** a coconut cake.
They **aren't going to paddle** in the ocean.
He **isn't going to stay** in a hotel.

	Eleni	Alex
pack a suitcase		
stay in a hotel		
go to the swimming pool		
paddle in the ocean		
go snorkeling		
put on sunscreen		

3 **Look at 2. Write sentences about Eleni and Alex's plans.**

Eleni: ➕ She's _____ .   Alex: ➕ _____ .
　　　 ➖ She isn't _____ .   　　　 ➖ _____ .

4 💬 **Act out and play *Guess what I'm going to do*.**

"You're going to go snorkeling …"　　"No. I'm going to put on sunscreen."

Talk buddies

I can talk about future plans and intentions.

85

**LESSON 4
Story**

The perfect vacation

1 Look. What is Ezra's mom's job?

2 🎧 Listen and read. Why is Ezra excited at the start of the story?

① My mom's a doctor and she works really hard. Next week we're going to go on vacation. We're going to catch a plane and stay in a hotel with a swimming pool near the beach! I am so excited – I have a big list of things I want to do.

② On our first day I say, "What are we going to do? There's kayaking, boat trips, surfing … Let's go snorkeling and I can use my new underwater camera…"
"Stop, Ezra," says my mom, "I'm going to relax on the beach and do nothing!"
"Oh, OK," I say.

③ Every day I show mom my list of activities and she says, "Not today, I'm going to relax." I don't understand! It's so boring – mom just lies there. I paddle in the ocean and go tide pooling. I see other people doing activities together, and it makes me sad.

Think!
Which picture do you think the monkey took?
Go to to page 125 to find out!

86

4 I'm bored lying on the beach! Then we talk about how tiring her job is. I try to relax. I do nothing. It feels good! I see the blue ocean and hear the wind in the palm trees. I start to understand why mom needs to relax …

"Hey!" A monkey took my camera! It climbs up a palm tree and throws it into the ocean!

Mom gives me a snorkeling mask.

"Come on," she says, "Let's find the camera."

We have an amazing time snorkeling around the coral reef looking for my camera, and mom finds it!

5 "Now I understand why you want to do this," says my mom, "You love being active and exploring! It's fun!"

The rest of the week we do activities in the morning, and relax in the afternoon. It's the perfect vacation!

3 Read again and complete.

1. Ezra wants to go _____ to use his camera.
2. Ezra's mom wants to _____ .
3. Ezra's mom has a _____ job.
4. A monkey takes _____ .

4 Think and answer.

1. Why does Ezra feel sad?
2. When does Ezra start to understand his mom's feelings?
3. When does Ezra's mom understand his point of view?

5 Act out the story. Then reflect.

Reflect
How do you understand other people's points of view?

Let's go snorkeling …

Stop, Ezra, … I'm going to relax on the beach.

Storytellers

I can read a story about different points of view.

LESSON 5
Vocabulary and Grammar

1 🎧 7.8 **Listen and say. Then tell a friend.**

1. go scuba diving

2. play beach volleyball

3. go on a boat trip

4. learn to surf

5. go tide pooling

6. go kayaking

Ways to learn

Put the activities in order for you.

1 = most favorite
→
6 = least favorite

2 🎧 7.9 **Listen, read, and check (✔).**

Carla: I'm going to go on vacation with my family this weekend.
Kai: Where are you going to go?
Carla: To a lake in the mountains.
Kai: Are you going to stay in a hotel?
Carla: No, we aren't. We're going to stay in an RV.
Kai: What are you going to do?
Carla: We're going to go kayaking.
Kai: Are you going to go snorkeling?
Carla: No, we aren't.
Kai: Are you going to play sports?
Carla: Yes, we are. We're going to play beach volleyball!

Grammar Heroes

What **are** you **going to do** in the summer?
I'm going to go on vacation.
Is she **going to** learn to surf?
Yes, she is.

3 💬 **Ask and answer about your next vacation.**

Where are you going to go?

I'm going to go to the beach.

Talk buddies

I can ask and answer about beach vacation activities.

LESSON 6
Listening and Speaking

1 ▶ Watch the video and write answers.

1. Where is Moana going to go?
   _____
2. Is she going to walk on the sand?
   _____
3. Is she going to help the baby turtle?
   _____
4. Is she going to fall into the ocean?
   _____

2 🎧 Listen, read, and check (✔) the online survey. What is Kai going to do?

What are you going to do at summer camp?

1. Are you going to learn to surf? ◯
2. Are you going to go on a boat trip? ◯
3. Are you going to go tide pooling? ◯
4. Are you going to play beach volleyball? ◯
5. Are you going to go scuba diving? ◯

Let's communicate!

3 💬 Check (✔) the questions for you. Then ask and answer.

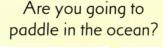 Are you going to paddle in the ocean?

 Yes, I am

 Go online
Communication Kit

I can use an online survey to talk about vacation plans.

LESSON 7
Myself and others

Understanding other people

1 Lessons 1 and 4   **Think and number in order.**

1.
a) Moana's mom says that her dad had a scary experience in the ocean. ☐
b) Moana's dad wants her to stay on the island. She doesn't understand why. ☐
c) Moana understands that her dad wants to keep her safe. ☐

2.
a) Ezra tries to relax and enjoys it. ☐
b) Ezra thinks it's boring just lying on the beach. ☐
c) He talks to his mom and understands she's tired and needs to relax. ☐

2 **Choose person A or B. Look at the picture. Write three things they think about the vacation.**

Person A
Likes: reading, hiking, kayaking
Typical vacations: camping in the wild

Person B
Likes: watching TV, playing video games, relaxing
Typical vacation: hotels near the beach

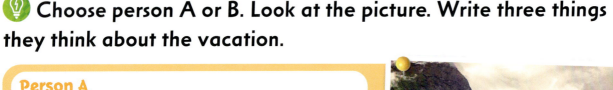

3 **Look at 2 and act out.**

I love this vacation because I want to be active on vacation.

I don't like it. I like relaxing and staying in hotels.

Useful Language
I think / want to … because …
What about you?
I understand why you feel that way.

4 **Read and think. Is this always true? Why?**

Just because you're right, doesn't mean I'm wrong.

Be a hero!
Talk about your favorite vacation. Can you understand your friend's point of view?

Social awareness I can understand and talk about different points of view.

90

Oceans, tides and waves

LESSON 8
My world

1 Watch the video and circle.

The wind makes **storms** / **tides** / **waves**.

2 Explore Read, listen, and circle.

a. There are five **oceans** / **seas**.
b. There is a force called **fall** / **gravity**.
c. Gravity makes **tides** / **waves**.
d. High tide is when the ocean levels **fall** / **rise**.

Oceans

There are five oceans on the Earth that cover almost 71% of the planet: the Atlantic Ocean, the Pacific Ocean, the Indian Ocean, the Southern Ocean, the Arctic Ocean. Smaller parts of these oceans are called seas.

Waves

The wind makes ocean water move in **waves**. Winds cause waves. The more wind, the bigger the waves. Large waves in ocean water usually come from stormy weather. The waves travel until they arrive on land.

wind
wave arriving on land

Tides

Sometimes you can visit a beach and the ocean is far away and there's lots of sand. Other times you can visit the same beach and the ocean is really close. This is because of the **tide**. Tides are the **rise** and **fall** of the ocean. There is a force called "**gravity**" between the Moon and Earth. The Moon's gravity pulls the oceans on Earth and makes the tides. On the side of Earth closest to the Moon, the water rises. This is because the Moon is pulling the water toward it. The ocean rises on the opposite side of Earth, too. This is because the Moon pulls Earth away from the water on the opposite side. These rises in ocean levels make a **high tide**. The other sides of Earth have a **low tide**.

Moon's gravity

Try it!
Create waves in water. How can you make waves bigger?

3 Think Read again and label the diagram.

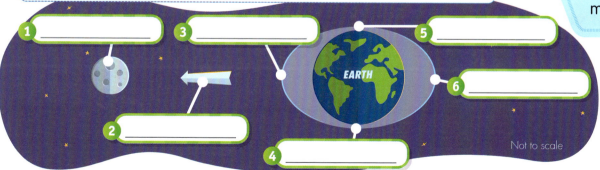

Not to scale

gravity
high tide (x2)
low tide (x2)
Moon

I can read and understand about the ocean.

91

LESSON 9
Project

A vacation collage

1 (Review) **Listen and write. What's missing from the picture?**

Our vacation island is going to have…

… a lovely 1 _sandy beach_ and 2 _____ . We have a large hotel with a 3 _____ and a colorful 4 _____ in the ocean.

Our amazing vacation island.

What are we going to do on our island?

You can go on a quiet boat trip, go 5 _____ around the coral reef or go 6 _____ ! You can learn to surf and play 7 _____ , too!

2 (Get ready) **In groups, share your ideas.**

What are you going to have on your island?

What activities are you going to do on your island?

Tips
Collaboration

- ☐ To make a group list, use a large piece of paper. Each student has a different color marker.
- ☐ Write your idea on the paper closest to you.
- ☐ Turn the paper around. Read what the other students wrote and write another idea.

3 (Create) **Make your group list and create a collage of your vacation island.** Workbook page 85

We're going to have an amazing beach. We're going to go tide pooling.

Writing: collage
- Write captions for the pictures on your collage. Make full sentences.
- Use describing words to explain clearly.

4   **Share your collage with the class.**

I can create a vacation collage.

LESSON 10 Review

1 Look and complete with *going to*.

1. What _____ do?
   + She _____ snorkeling.
   − She _____ kayaking.

2. What _____ ?
   + They _____ .
   − They _____ .

Movie challenge
How many things on Moana's island can you say in 30 seconds? Go!

2 Imagine you are going on vacation. What are you going to do? Write. _____

_____

3 💬 Compare Ezra's vacation plans with your list in 2. Then tell a friend.

I'm going on vacation next week. I'm going to walk on the sand and paddle in the ocean. I'm going to go tide pooling. I'm going to go to the swimming pool. I'm going to play beach volleyball.

Ezra's going to walk on the sand, I'm not going to walk on the sand.

Sticker time

I can ...
- 💬 name and identify beach and vacation activities ☐
- 📖 read a story ☐
- 🎨 design a vacation collage ☐
- 🧠 understand different points of view ☐

✅ **I completed Unit 7!**

Extra Lesson

Go online Big Project

93

8 Awesome cities

What world cities do you know? Share ideas.

skyscraper

Video story

downtown

1 🎬 Watch the video. Check (✔). What does Hiro create first?

1 2 3 4

2 🎬 Watch again and answer.

1. Why does Hiro need a schedule?
2. What does Hiro brainstorm with his friends?
3. Where does Hiro make his plans for the superhero costumes?

94

LESSON 1 Vocabulary

3 🎧 8.1 Listen, find, and say. Then tell a friend.

1 2 3 4

4 🎵 8.2 Listen, chant, and act.

Welcome to my awesome city!
The skyscrapers are tall and pretty.
Highways cross with lots of cars,
As people visit from near and far.
Here's the university,
That's where I study!
It's exciting walking downtown,
Come on! Let's look around!

5 💬 Play *Guess the city place*.

Is it a skyscraper?

No, it isn't. Guess again!

Talk buddies

university

highway

I can name places in a city.

95

LESSON 2
Vocabulary

1 🎧 8.3 **Listen and say. Then tell a friend.**

1 modern

2 historic

3 beautiful

4 awesome

5 expensive

6 interesting

7 famous

8 unusual

2 🎧 8.4 **Listen and add a describing word.**

3 **Look, read, and match.**

1. This city has a modern bridge and historic buildings.
2. These awesome buildings look like trees. They are beautiful!
3. This city has lots of highways and modern skyscrapers.
4. This city is famous for its unusual and colorful buildings.

Guess what?
San Fransokyo in *Big Hero 6* looks like two real cities: San Francisco and Tokyo.

a

b

c

d

4 💬 **Write about a place in your town. Then play *Guess the place*.**

Talk buddies

It's beautiful and historic. It's near the park.

It's beautiful and historic. It's near the park.

The university!

I can describe cities.

96

LESSON 3
Grammar

1 🎧 8.5 **Listen, read, and circle.**

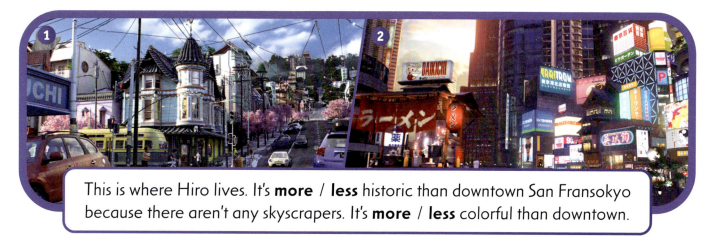

This is where Hiro lives. It's **more** / **less** historic than downtown San Fransokyo because there aren't any skyscrapers. It's **more** / **less** colorful than downtown.

2 🎧 8.6 **Listen and match.**

Grammar Heroes
I think old buildings are **more beautiful** than modern buildings.
Rome is **less modern** than Shanghai.

ⓐ Kyoto ☐
ⓑ Tokyo ☐

3 🎧 8.7 **Listen again and write.**

① Tokyo is _____ (famous) than Kyoto.

② Kyoto is _____ (modern) Tokyo.

③ I think Kyoto _____ (beautiful) Tokyo.

④ Kyoto _____ (historic) Tokyo.

4 💬 **Play Sentence chain.**

Mexico City is more modern than Veracruz.

I think Veracruz is more beautiful than New York.

I can talk about and compare cities.

LESSON 4
Story

The city design competition

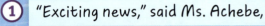

1 Look. What is the competition?

2 🎧 8.8 Listen and read. What green space does Carla's team's building have?

Competition: Design a city building

Make a model of your building. Think about these questions:
- Where is your building?
- What type of building is it? Why?
- What green space can you add?

① "Exciting news," said Ms. Achebe, "There's a school competition to design a building."

② All the children entered the competition. Carla, Kai, and Eleni made a team.

"Let's make a plan," said Carla, "First, let's brainstorm ideas."

Carla wanted a modern skyscraper. Kai wanted a university building.

"Remember we need some green space. We could have a living wall and a roof garden!" said Carla.

"Yes! Let's make a list of all the things we need and the things we want," said Eleni.

"It's a long list!" said Kai, "Do we have time?"

"Let's make a schedule and decide what to do first," said Carla.

③ The next day, Kai looked at the other team. "Ezra's team have a model already! It's awesome."

"Oooh ..." said Carla, "They worked quickly!"

Every day, Ezra's team added more amazing things to their model.

Think!
Which do you think is Carla's team's design?
Go to to page 126 to find out!

98

4 It was the day of the competition. Ezra's team's design was bigger and more beautiful. "They are going to win," said Carla, "It's the most unusual and modern design."
Ezra's team presented their design to the judges first.
"It's unusual and modern, but where's the green space?" asked a judge.
"Oh, we didn't plan that," said Ezra.
"Erm … it can go here," said Alex quickly.
"Hmm. OK," said the judge.

5 Carla's team presented their design. The teams nervously waited to find out the winner. "Congratulations Carla, Kai, and Eleni! You win the prize! Your skyscraper was the most beautiful and the best planned!"

3 Read again and complete.

1. Carla wanted to design a _____ .
2. Carla wanted a living wall and a _____ .
3. _____'s team made their model first.
4. Carla's team won the _____ .

4 Think and answer.

1. What does Carla's team do first?
2. Why does Carla make a schedule?
3. What makes you think Ezra's team didn't plan very well?

5 💬 **Act out the story. Then reflect.**

Reflect
How do you organize yourself and make plans?

Storytellers

Let's make a plan … let's brainstorm ideas.

Let's make a schedule.

I can read a story about planning and organizing.

LESSON 5
Vocabulary and Grammar

1 🎧 8.9 **Listen and say. Then tell a friend.**

 1 office building

 2 elevator

 3 railroad tracks

 4 living wall

 5 roof garden

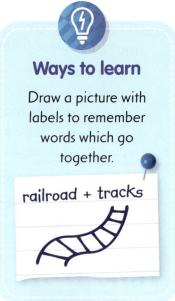

Ways to learn
Draw a picture with labels to remember words which go together.

railroad + tracks

2 🎧 8.10 **Listen, read, and write.**

Carla: I think city downtowns are the least beautiful places.

Ezra: Not always! Look at these pictures. There are lots of ways to make downtowns more beautiful.

Carla: Oh, yes! Those roof gardens are the most beautiful spaces!

Ezra: Look at that building with a living wall. They're the most modern idea.

Carla: That looks amazing! I love the skyscraper with glass elevators, too. Look at that highway. I think the best way to make cities more beautiful is to plant flowers and plants along highways and railroad tracks.

the best   the most beautiful
the most modern

Grammar Heroes

Roof gardens are **the most beautiful** green spaces in cities.
Universities are sometimes **the least historic** buildings in cities.

3 💬 **Play Most / least.**

Roof gardens are the most beautiful.

Railroad tracks are the least beautiful.

Talk buddies

I can describe things in cities.

100

LESSON 6
Listening and Speaking

1 Watch the video and circle.

1. San Fransokyo has the **least** / **most** modern skyscrapers and office buildings.
2. The bad guy does the most **amazing** / **unusual** jump over a bridge.
3. GoGo is the **slowest** / **most awesome** driver.

2 Listen and complete the *Amazing City* fact cards.

The _____ hotel in the world!
Name: Marina Bay Sands Hotel
Country: Singapore
Amazing fact: The hotel has the _____ swimming pool in the world.

The _____ living wall in the world!
Name: _____ del Claustro de Sor Juana
Country: Mexico
Amazing fact: There's a _____ on the living wall.

Let's communicate!

3 Make an *Amazing City* fact card. Ask and answer.

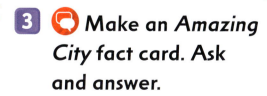

Go online
Communication Kit

What's the most frightening elevator in the world?

I think it's the Bailong Elevator in China.

I can use fact cards to describe and compare cities.

101

LESSON 7
Myself and others

Let's make plans!

1 Lessons 1 and 4 — Think and match. What do they do to make a plan?

a) Brainstorm ideas. ☐
b) Make a list. ☐
c) Decide what to do first. ☐
d) Make a schedule. ☐

2 What could Ryan do to plan? Share ideas. Then listen. Does his friend have the same ideas as you?

> I need to design a roof garden for my school project. I don't know where to start.

3 Complete the "to do" list and add your ideas. Put each action on a schedule.

Project:
Create a city picture poster

To do list
- Take pictures of _____
- Find out about _____
- Stick _____
- Choose _____
- _____
- _____

Monday	Tuesday	Wednesday	Thursday	Friday
___	___	___	___	Present city picture poster

Useful Language
Let's plan. What are we going to do?
What should we do first?
First, / Then we could …

4 Share your ideas. Did your friends have different ideas? How did they make their plan?

Help a friend make a plan for something important.

Self-management I can recognize ways to plan and organize.

Cities

LESSON 8
Design **My world**

1 ▶ Watch the video and circle.

Most of the skyscrapers in downtown San Fransokyo are **apartments** / **office buildings** / **universities**.

2 🎧 **Explore** Read, listen, and circle.

City Design

a) **Bicycle lanes** / **Overpasses** take cars away from downtown.
b) A sustainable city helps the **environment** / **transportation system**.

Buildings
There are many different types of buildings in cities. There are homes, offices, schools, universities, and stores. Usually, office buildings and stores are in the downtown area of a city. Modern office and apartment buildings are often in skyscrapers.

Transportation systems
The **transportation system** in a city is very important. Cities with busy highways are more dangerous. Highways and railroad tracks that go over the city on **overpasses** or under the city in tunnels take cars away from downtown. Quieter highways are better for the environment, too, because more people can walk and ride their bikes safely. Special parts of the street which are only for cyclists, are called **bicycle lanes**.

Sustainable Cities
People need places to live, work, and go to school, but the most important thing in modern cities is the green spaces.
A **sustainable** city helps the **environment**. Birds, animals, and insects need plants, trees, and water. All cities have parks, but what are **city planners** doing to make modern sustainable features in cities? Some unusual ideas are: living walls with plants on the outside of skyscrapers, and modern fountains in town squares and parks.

Try it!
Walk around your city. Make a list of what you want to change.

3 💡 **Think** Add transportation systems and sustainable features. Share your ideas.

I put in an overpass with a highway. It takes cars away from downtown.

I made a green space with a water feature.

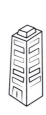
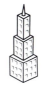

I can read and understand about city design.

LESSON 9
Project

A pop-up city map

1 🎧 8.14 (Review) Look and match. Then listen and check (✓) the places Kai talks about.

- ① balcony
- ○ elevator
- ○ overpass
- ○ highway

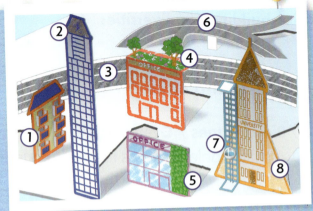

- ○ living wall
- ○ roof garden
- ○ skyscraper
- ○ university

① The university is the most unusual building in the city.
② This office building is more modern than the skyscraper. It has a living wall.

2 (Get ready) Choose places for your city.

What sustainable features can your city have?

Tips
Self-management
- ☐ Make a list of what you want to include on your map.
- ☐ Use pictures to help you to remember new words.

3 (Create) Make a list and create your map. **Workbook** page 97

4 (Share) Share your pop-up city map with the class.

Writing: map
- Compare things in your city using *more* and *the most*.
- Write in full sentences. Use your most beautiful handwriting!

I can create a pop-up city map.

I can do it!

LESSON 10 Review

1 🎧 **Listen and write. Then match.**

1. This is one of the _____ in the world!
2. This is the _____ in Europe. It's also one of the _____ in Europe.
3. Many people think this is _____ city in the world. It's very _____ .

 a

 b

 c

Movie challenge
How many features of San Fransokyo can you describe in 30 seconds? Go!

2 **Write about San Fransokyo.**

This is San Fransokyo. It's **1** _____ city!

The skyscrapers are **2** _____ than the **3** _____ in my city.

It's less **4** _____ than my city.

Sticker time

I can ...

- 💬 name and describe places in cities ☐
- 📖 read a story ☐
- 🎨 create a pop-up city map ☐
- 💡 make plans and be organized ☐

✓ **I completed Unit 8!**

105

9 One planet

What do you do to help the planet? Share ideas.

garbage

Video story

1. Watch the video. Check (✓). Who lives on Earth?

2. Watch again and answer.
   1. Why did the people leave Earth?
   2. What does WALL-E do?
   3. What does WALL-E reuse?

tire

LESSON 1 **Vocabulary**

3 🎧 **Listen, find, and say. Then tell a friend.**

4 🎵 **Listen, chant, and act.**

There's a lot of garbage, what can we do?
We can recycle things and save the planet, too!
Recycle that bottle, recycle those cans,
It's a good plan!

There's a lot of garbage, what can we do?
We can reuse things and save the planet, too!
Reuse that tire, reuse those cards.
It's not hard!

5 💬 **What do you put in the garbage? Share ideas.**

We put a lot of plastic bottles in the garbage.

We put cans in the garbage.

Talk buddies

bottle

can

I can name things you throw out.

107

LESSON 2
Vocabulary

1 🎧 9.3 **Listen and say. Then tell a friend.**

1 recycle newspapers   2 turn off the lights   3 pick up trash   4 reuse plastic bags

5 litter   6 waste water   7 throw out garbage   8 pollute the air

2 🎧 9.4 💬 **Listen and say. Then play *Word chain*.**

3 **Look, read, and match. Then write sentences.**

1 I'm going to use these plastic bags again for the shopping.
2 I'm going to ride my bike to school so that I don't go in the car.
3 I'm going to take showers, not baths.

Guess what?
We waste around a third of the food we grow and make.

 a    b    c

I'm not going to pollute the air. _____ _____

4 💬 **Write a plan to help the planet. Then share ideas.**

I'm going to recycle cans. I'm going to pick up trash ...

I'm going to recycle cans.

That's a good idea. I'm going to turn off the lights.

Talk buddies

I can name actions that are good and bad for the planet.

LESSON 3
Grammar

1 🎧 9.5 **Listen, read, and match.**

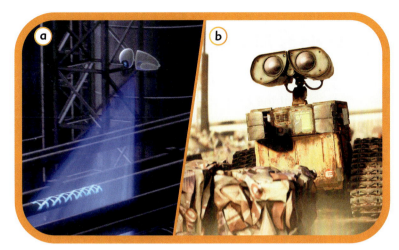

1. This robot must pick up the trash.
2. This robot can't stop looking for a plant.
3. This robot isn't allowed to leave planet Earth.

2 🎧 9.6 **Read and circle. Then listen and check.**

Grammar Heroes
You **must** recycle cans and plastic bottles.
We **can't** waste electricity.
I'**m not allowed** to throw plastic bottles in the trash.
---

1. You **can't** / **must** turn off the faucet.
2. You **can't** / **must** waste water.
3. You **can't** / **must** always go to school in the car.
4. We'**re not allowed to** / **must** walk to school by ourselves.
5. We **can't** / **must** run to the bus stop.
6. We **aren't allowed to** / **must** be late for school!

3 Look at the words in Lesson 2. Write for you.

1 I must _____ .
2 I can't _____ .
3 I'm not allowed to _____ .

4 💬 What class rules do you have? Share ideas.

We must recycle or reuse paper.

We aren't allowed to eat in class.

Talk buddies

I can talk about rules.

109

LESSON 4 Story

CARLA'S PENPAL

1 Look. What does Carla do after school?

2 🎧 9.7 Listen and read. What year does Mia come from?

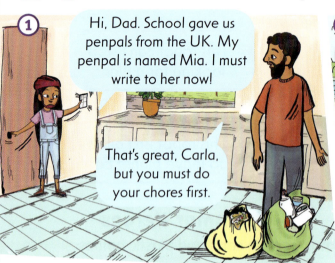

① Hi, Dad. School gave us penpals from the UK. My penpal is named Mia. I must write to her now!

That's great, Carla, but you must do your chores first.

② Carla does her chores quickly. She throws out the garbage, but she doesn't recycle the plastic and glass bottles, and cans.

③ Carla opens her laptop so that she can write to Mia.

Hi Mia, I'm Carla. I go to Park School. I love growing plants and walking by the river.

Pleased to meet you, Carla. Wow! You're allowed to go to school! And what are "plants" and "rivers"?

You do speak English, right?!

④ Mia?!

I came to see these things for myself.

I don't understand. How …

⑤ All those green things — what are they? And is that water?

They're grass and trees! The water is a river. You have them in the UK.

We don't have them in the year 3021!

In the future?!

Think!
What does Mia's world look like?
Go to to page 127 to find out!

3 Read again and write answers.

1. What activities does Carla like doing?
   _____

2. What doesn't Mia have in her world?
   _____

3. Do you think Mia really visited Carla?
   _____

4 Think and answer.

1. How does Carla help the planet?
2. What does Mia say people must do to save the planet?
3. What do you think Mia could do with the plants?

5 Act out the story. Then reflect.

Reflect
What do you do to help the planet?

… you must recycle, and reduce waste.

Don't waste water and electricity …

Storytellers

I can read a story about helping the planet.

LESSON 5
Vocabulary and Grammar

1 🎧 9.8 **Listen and say. Then tell a friend.**

 1 have fresh air

 2 stop pollution

 3 save electricity

 4 use less gasoline

 5 reduce waste

 6 keep the planet clean

Ways to learn
Put the actions in order for you.

1 = most important
↓
6 = least important

2 🎧 9.9 **Listen, read, and write E (Eleni) or K (Kai).**

Kai: Did you enjoy WALL-E, Eleni?

Eleni: Yes, I did. It's a great movie, but I'm worried. I don't want a future like that.

Kai: Yes, it's scary. We must recycle more so that we reduce waste.

Eleni: Yes, and we can't litter. We don't want trash to go into the oceans!

Kai: We must turn off lights and faucets so that we save electricity and don't waste water.

Eleni: Yes, and we can plant more trees so that we have more fresh air.

Kai: We can't let it be like WALL-E's world!

a
b
c

Grammar Heroes
We can recycle more cans **so that** there is less trash.
We must use cars less **so that** we reduce pollution.

3 💬 **Why do you do things to help the planet?**

I reuse things so that we throw out less garbage.

I take a shower so that I save water.

 Talk buddies

I can give reasons for actions to help the planet.

 Extra Lesson

 Go online Phonics

LESSON 6
Listening and Speaking

1 🎬 9B Watch the video and write answers.

① EVE reuses the tracks so that _____.

② She fixes WALL-E's eyes so that _____.

③ The baby waters the plant so that _____.

④ The people must plant more plants so that _____.

2 🎧 9.10 Read and match the playing cards. Then listen and check.

1. Recycle plastic so that …
2. Buy less food so that …
3. Ride a bike or walk to school so that …
4. Turn off the faucet so that …

a. you use less gasoline.
b. you don't waste water.
c. you reduce food waste.
d. you reduce pollution in the oceans.

Let's communicate!

3 💬 Make cards. Then play *Find and match*.

Go online
Communication Kit

Pick up trash so that …

…there's less trash in the streets!

I can use playing cards to talk about helping the planet.

113

LESSON 7
Myself and others

Making a difference!

1    Think and match. How do they help the planet?

a Pick up trash.
b Recycle or reuse things.
c Grow plants.
d Ride a bike to school.

2 Complete the quiz.

Are you an Eco Warrior?

❶ You have an old glass bottle. Do you …
 a recycle it?
 b reuse it?
 c throw it in the trash?

❷ You see some metal cans on the ground in the park. Do you …
 a take them home to recycle?
 b put them in the trash?
 c leave them?

❸ What do you do about pollution?
 a Ride a bike or walk to more places.
 b Take buses, trains, or the subway.
 c Nothing. I go everywhere by car.

❹ What's the most important thing you can do to help the planet?
 a Recycle, reduce, and reuse.
 b Plant trees.
 c Nothing.

Your score:
Mostly As and Bs: Good job! You are an Eco Warrior.
Mostly Cs: Remember we only have one planet! You must do more to help!

3  How can you help the planet? Share ideas.

At home   At school   In your neighborhood

Useful Language
I think we must …
We could …

4 Decide and write the top three class promises to the planet.

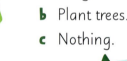
We're going to recycle more.

Be a hero!
Keep a diary of how you help the planet.

Responsible decision-making I can recognize ways to make a difference.

Garbage

LESSON 8
My world

1 **Watch the video and circle.**

WALL-E's box is made of **metal / plastic / gold**.

2 **Explore** Read, listen, and number.

What do we do with garbage?

We throw out garbage every day. It pollutes the planet. How much garbage does your family make in a year? It's a lot! What can we do?

❶ Burn it

We can **burn** garbage. But things like plastic bags and tires pollute the air when they burn. This isn't good because living things need fresh air.

❷ Put it in landfill

Landfill is a big hole in the ground for garbage. Trash that goes into landfill can pollute the land and water. Living things can **die** in polluted water.

What are better things to do with garbage?

❸ Biodegrade

A lot of our garbage is food waste from the kitchen. Food waste biodegrades. Garden waste biodegrades, too. Tiny living things make things biodegrade. Don't throw out **biodegradable** waste in the garbage. Waste from non-living things like plastic and metal is **non-biodegradable**.

❹ Recycle

We can recycle lots of non-biodegradable garbage like glass bottles, plastic bottles, card, and metal cans. Recycled card and paper make new paper, and recycled glass bottles make new glass bottles. Some recycled things make something different, for example, plastic bottles can make clothes!

a
b
c
d

3 **Think** Read again and sort.

apple   glass bottle   grass   metal can   plastic bottle

Biodegrades: _____ , _____
Recycle: _____ , _____ , _____

Try it!
Put one apple core in the sunlight and one in the dark. How are they different after two weeks?

I can read and understand about garbage.

LESSON 9 Project

A picture diary

1   **Review** Listen and write *First, Next* or *Then*.

Save electricity!
1 _____, I turned off the lights.

You can't litter!
2 _____, I picked up trash with my family.

We must reduce waste!
3 _____, I recycled metal cans.

A fun weekend!
The next day, I planted trees in my neighbourhood.

2 **Get ready** In groups, decide what things you can do.

> We could pick up trash in the street.

> I'm going to walk to school.

3 **Create** Create your picture diary.

Workbook page 109

 Writing: picture diary
- Use **First**, **Next**, and **Then** to write what you did in order.
- Write a short caption for each picture.

4 **Share** Present your picture diary.

Tips
Presentation
- ☐ Create a presentation card for each picture.
- ☐ Don't read from your cards – use them as a reminder.
- ☐ Point to the picture you're talking about.

I can create a picture diary.

LESSON 10 Review

I can do it!

1 Read and complete with *must*, *can't*, and *not allowed*.

Our Eco Rules!

1. We _____ waste electricity – turn off lights!
2. We're _____ to throw food waste in the trash.
3. We _____ recycle paper, glass, cans, and plastic.
4. We _____ pick up trash.
5. We _____ litter!
6. We _____ save our planet!

2 Look at 1. Act out and play *Guess the rule*.

You're not allowed to throw food waste in the trash?

Yes!

Movie challenge
How many garbage things in *WALL-E* can you say in 30 seconds? Go!

3 Write things you *must*, *can't*, and *aren't allowed* to do at home.

_____
_____
_____

Sticker time

I can ...
- name and identify ways to help the planet ☐
- read a story ☐
- present a picture diary ☐
- make a difference by helping the planet ☐

✓ I completed Unit 9!

Test your progress with English Benchmark Young Learners

Grammar

1 Dates

When we write or say dates, we often use ordinal numbers.

When we write dates using only the ordinal number, we add 'the' before the number.

What's	the date	today?
		on Saturday?
It's	June 3rd.	
	the 10th.	

We can use dates with 'on' for days of the week, dates in the calendar, or special dates like birthdays.

When's	your	birthday?
My birthday is	on Tuesday.	
	on October 2nd.	

When's your birthday?

It's September 7th.

Vocabulary

1 🎧 10.1 Ordinal numbers

1st 2nd 3rd 4th 5th

6th 7th 8th 9th 10th

first   second   third

fourth   fifth   sixth

seventh   eighth   ninth   tenth

2 Months

January   February   March

April   May   June   July

August   September   October

November   December

118

1

Grammar

1 Routine activities

He/She	always	wears a helmet on his/her bike.
I/We/They	never	play video games.
I/We/They	do	my/our/their homework every day.

2 Activities happening now

Look! He**'s winning** the race.
They**'re crossing** the finishing line.
Oh, no! I**'m not wearing** my helmet!

3 Making suggestions

I/You He/She We/They	could	enter	the competition.
		go	across the bridge.

Think!

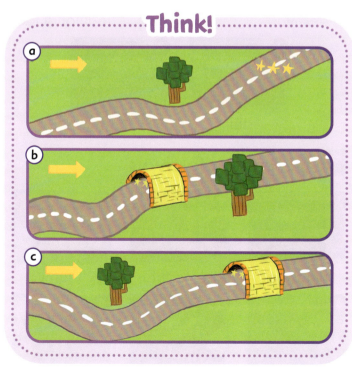

Answer: c

Vocabulary

1 🎧 10.2 Actions in a competition

cross the finish line

win a trophy

get a medal

start a race

2 Actions in a race

wear a helmet

win a prize

score points

fall over

lose a race

take part

go through a tunnel

cheer for the winner

3 Obstacles on a racetrack

into the net

along the racetrack

around the cones

across the bridge

over the hill

past the flags

2

Grammar

1 Wh– questions

Where was the festival.
It **was** in the town square.
Why were the floats in the street?
Because there **was** a festival.
When were the fireworks?
They **were** in the evening.

2 Yes/No questions + adjectives

Was it colorful?
Yes, it **was**. No, it **wasn't**.
Were they amazing?
Yes, they **were**. No, they **weren't**.

Think!

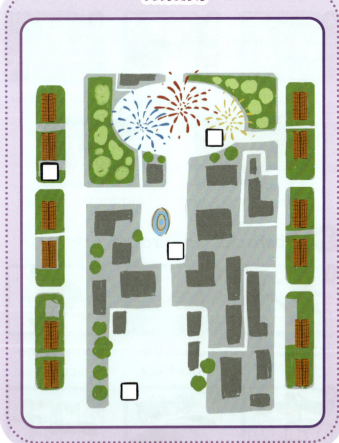

Answer: town square → fountain → Kai's street → next to the park

Vocabulary

1 🎧 10.3 Things in the town center

town square

palace

fountain

people

2 Things at festivals

fireworks

float

parade

festival

costume

traditional food

stall

lantern

3 Describing festivals

amazing

colorful

fun

awful

noisy

scary

3

Grammar

1 good at / not good at

She's **good at** ice-skating.
We're **not good at** doing gymnastics **yet**.

2 Adverbs

To make adverbs add *-ly* to the end of adjectives.
bad ➜ bad**ly**
safe ➜ safe**ly**
quick ➜ quick**ly**
careful ➜ careful**ly**
Add *-ily* to the end of adjectives ending in y.
happy ➜ happ**ily**

Irregular adverbs

good ➜ **well**

Think!

a, b, c, d, e

Answer: a vision (a little), c hearing, e touch

Vocabulary

1 🎧 10.4 Sports activities

1 hitting a puck   2 trampolining

3 playing ice hockey   4 ice skating

2 More sports

1 snowboarding   2 doing gymnastics   3 cycling

4 skateboarding   5 roller skating   6 playing baseball

7 playing badminton   8 playing tennis

3 Adverbs

1 quickly   2 slowly   3 carefully

4 safely   5 badly   6 well

121

Grammar

1 Comparatives

smart → smart**er than**
fast → fast**er than**
large → larg**er than**
fierce → fierc**er than**
happy → happ**ier than**
tiny → tin**ier than**
big → big**ger than**

Irregular comparatives

good → better
bad → worse

2 Superlatives

small → **the** small**est**
fast → **the** fast**est**
fierce → **the** fierc**est**
tiny → **the** tin**iest**
big → **the** big**gest**

Irregular superlatives

good → better → the best
bad → worse → the worst

Think!

a
b
c

Answer: c

Vocabulary

1 Animals 10.5

buffalo

otter

cheetah

hippo

2 Describing animals

cute

hairy

large

friendly

tiny

fierce

smart

furry

3 More animals

sloth

shrew

wolf

panda

polar bear

yak

122

Grammar

1 Simple Past: regular verbs

arrive → arriv**ed**
farm → farm**ed**
hunt → hunt**ed**
travel → travel**ed**
carry → carr**ied***

*carry → carry → carr**ied**

Positive / Negative

I/You/He/She/They	lived in huts.

I/You He/She We/They	didn't	travel to Mexico. use a pencil. carry our backpacks.

2 Simple Past: questions

Did	you she they	sail a boat? live in the city? start a fire?
Yes, I/she/they did.		No, I/she/they didn't.

Think!

Answer: b

Vocabulary

1 🎧 10.6 Things from the past

port   hut

carriage   ship

2 Actions in the past

farm   hunt   carry

travel   sail   visit

pick   use

3 More things from the past

pyramid   corn   basket

oven   spear   bow and arrow

123

Grammar

1 Simple Past: irregular verbs

do → did	see → saw
eat → ate	sleep → slept
fall → fell	steal → stole
find → found	swim → swam
get → got	take → took
go → went	tell → told
have → had	win → won
make → made	write → wrote

2 Simple Past: irregular verbs

Where	did	you he/she they	go	on the weekend?
What			do	in the video game?

Did	you	find	a fossil?	Yes, I/we did
				No, I/we didn't.

Think!

a, b, c

Answer: c

Vocabulary

1 🎧 10.7 Outdoor activities

do archery

go rock climbing

eat outdoors

catch fish

2 Outdoor activities

swim outdoors

go on an adventure

build a den

get lost

make a campfire

see wild animals

go mountain biking

go rafting

3 More outdoor activities

find fossils

go stargazing

catch a leaf

throw stones in a stream

explore a cave

see the sunset / sunrise

7

Grammar

1 Future plans, intentions, and predictions

He/She's	going to	walk on the sand	tomorrow.
I'm			this afternoon.
We're		pack my suitcase	next week.
			on vacation.

| It's | going to | rain. |
| We aren't | | get lost. |

2 Questions about plans, intentions, and predictions

| Are you | going to | stay in a hotel? |
| Is he/she | | go on a boat trip? |

| Yes, I am. | No, I'm not. |
| Yes, he/she is. | No, he/she isn't. |

| Is the tour | going to | start soon? |

| Yes, it is. | No, it isn't. |

Think!

Answer: c

Vocabulary

1 🎧 10.8 Things on an island

coconuts

coral reef

island

palm trees

2 Beach vacation activities

walk on the sand

pack a suitcase

catch a plane

go to the swimming pool

paddle in the ocean

stay in a hotel

put on sunscreen

go snorkeling

3 More beach vacation activities

go scuba diving

play beach volleyball

go on a boat trip

learn to surf

go tide pooling

go kayaking

125

8

Grammar

1 Comparatives

My city	is	more exciting than	your village.
My new apartment		less modern than	my old apartment.
Museums	are	more interesting than	universities.
Vacations		less boring than	staying at home.

2 Superlatives

That elevator is		frightening thing!
It's	the most the least	expensive book in the bookstore.
He/She's		famous person from our city. careful driver.

Think!

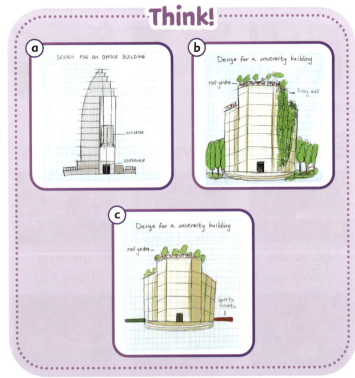

Answer: b

Vocabulary

1 🎧 10.9 Places in a city

skyscraper

university

highway

downtown

2 Describing cities

modern

historic

beautiful

awesome

expensive

interesting

famous

unusual

3 Things in cities

office building

elevator

railroad tracks

living wall

roof garden

balcony

126

9

Grammar

1 Obligation and permission

Rules for myself
I **must** pick up trash. = I want to pick up trash and it's the right thing to do.
We **can't** litter. = I don't want to litter, it's the wrong thing to do.

Rules from others
We **aren't allowed to** be late for class. = It's a class rule.
I'm not allowed to ride my bike to school. = My parents don't let me.

2 Reasons

We must ride a bike **so that** we don't use the car. = We must ride a bike **because** we don't want to use the car.
I turn off lights **so that** we save electricity. = I turn off lights **because** I want to save electricity.

Think!

a

b

c

Answer: a

Vocabulary

1 🎧 10.10 Things you throw out

garbage

can

bottle

tire

2 Good / bad things for the planet

recycle newspapers

turn off the lights

pick up trash

reuse plastic bags

litter

waste water   throw out garbage   pollute the air

3 Actions to help the planet

have fresh air

stop pollution

save electricity

use less gasoline

reduce waste

keep the planet clean

Pearson Education Limited
KAO Two
KAO Park
Hockham Way
Harlow, Essex
CM17 9SR
England
and Associated Companies throughout the world.

pearsonenglish.com
© Pearson Education Limited 2022

© 2022 Disney Enterprises, Inc. All rights reserved. Pixar properties © Disney/Pixar

The right of Mary Roulston to be identified as the author of this Work has been asserted by them in accordance with the Copyright, Designs and Patents Act 1988.

All rights reserved; no part of this publication may be reproduced, stored in a retrieval system, or transmitted in any form or by any means, electronic, mechanical, photocopying, recording, or otherwise without the prior written permission of the Publishers.

First published 2022
ISBN: 978-1-292-44171-9
Set in Arta Std Medium 17/22pt

Printed in Slovakia by Neografia

Acknowledgements:
The publishers and author would like to thank the following people for their feedback and comments during the development of the material: Maria Silvina Campagnoli, Maria Lidia Camporro, Maria Sol Diaz, Tatiana Fanshtein, Jiang Xin, Paula Mior, Anita Parlaj-Naranic, Marta Popiolek, Jelena Tosic.

Image Credits:
123RF.com: Aleksei Potov 71, 124, Alta Oosthuizen 47, 122, Andreanita 53, 52, 122, Cathy Yeulet 92, Dmytro Vietrov 116, Fazon 96, Georgy Kopytin 47, 122, HONGQI ZHANG 39, Khunaspix 107, 127, Kittinit Yassara 107, 127, Lightfieldstudios 28, 120, Lightpoet 107, 127, Martin PHOTOTRIP 56, Natallia Yaumenenka 52, 122, Olegdoroshin 71, 124, Orkhv 96, 126, Rumos 71, 124, Satina 100, 126, Sergey Novikov 88, 125, Soloway 35, 121, THANANIT SUNTIVIRIYANON 23, 120, Vladislav Zolotov 96, 126, Wan Rosli Wan Othman 71, 124, Wasin Pummarin 97; **Alamy Stock Photo:** 2d Alan King 61, Barry Diomede 71, 124, Ben McRae 49, Cavan Images 88, 125, Daniel Damaschin 28, 120, Ian Littlewood 23, 120, Jennika Argent 23, 120, Jimena Roquero 43, Jochen Tack 23, 120, Kamel ADJENEF 123, Lev Dolgachov 12, Matjaz Corel 76, 124, Prisma by Dukas Presseagentur GmbH 123, Robertharding 23, 120, Silvia Huelva-Photos of Spain 23, 120, Sorrorwoot Chaiyawong 105, Tetra Images 104; **Getty Images:** 3bugsmom 15, Aaaaimages 100, 126, Andersen Ross Photography Inc 60, AndreaObzerova 27, Andresr 54, Ariel Skelley 116, Astrakan Images 40, 121, Blend Images/Pete Saloutos 11, 119, Brusinski 63, Camille Tokerud 40, 121, Capuski 48, 122, CARL DE SOUZA 32, Catherine Delahaye 112, 127, Chinaface 95, 126, Choice76 115, Dan Brownsword 107, 127, Darrell Gulin 49, Davel5957 23, 120, David Madison 71, 124, Don Baird 48, 122, Dragos Cojocari 63, Drbimages 113, DuKai photographer 103, Dulyanut Swdp 100, 126, Eddy Zecchinon / EyeEm 76, 124, Eric Lafforgue/Art in All of Us 32, Eric Raptosh Photography 84, 125, FatCamera 43, 12, 119, Flashpop 48, Flojate 41, Galina Zhigalova / EyeEm 77, Gary John Norman 20, Goncharovaia 95, 126, Haitong Yu 83, 125, Hannes Eichinger / EyeEm 12, Hill Street Studios 96, 126, HRAUN 84, IAN HOOTON/SPL 84, 125, Imgorthand 81, 84, 125, Inside Creative House 24, IT Stock 100, 126, Jackal Pan 104, Jacobs Stock Photography Ltd 11, 119, Janie Airey 12, 119, 12, 119, JBryson 8, 87, JGI/Jamie Grill 48, Joe Daniel Price 96, JohnnyGreig 23, 120, Jon Feingersh 11, 119, Jose Luis Pelaez Inc 116, Jure Gasparic / EyeEm 77, Kali9 28, 120, Katiafonti 17, 113, Keith Brofsky 88, 125, Kerkez 71, 124, LSOphoto 48, MaFelipe 84, 125, Maica 76, 124, Maodesign 32, Marco Bottigelli 83, 125, Martin-dm 84, 125, Maskot 116, Matelly 8, Matt Carr 71, 124, MBI 80, Milko 41, Mint Images - Art Wolfe 47, 122, Moodboard 115, Morsa Images 8, 65, 111, Mypurgatoryyears 76, 124, Nachosuch 52, 122, Norbert Schaefer/Corbis 60, Ollo 112, 127, Ozgurdonmaz 29, Paul Biris 103, PeakSTOCK 89, Peter Cade 40, 121, Peter Dazeley 108, 127, Philippe LEJEANVRE 32, PhotoAlto/Anne-Sophie Bost 27, Plan Shoot / Imazins 108, Primeimages 59, 123, Ranplett 78, Richard Drury 76, 124, Rubberball/Mike Kemp 108, 127, RUSS ROHDE 108, 127, Sami Sarkis 88, 125, Schroptschop 108, 127, Sebastian Condrea 35, 121, Shank_ali 35, 121, Shannon Fagan 42, Shoji Fujita 43, 35, 121, Simonlong 32, Sirikorn Thamniyom / EyeEm 101, 108, Skyler Ewing / EyeEm 75, 96, Sola Deo Gloria 40, 121, SolStock 12, 119, Somethingway 8, Stanley45 29, StefaNikolic 71, 124, Steve Smith 35, 121, StockPlanets 40, 121, SunforRise 12, 127, Surasak Soottihikarn / EyeEm 15, Tatsiana Volkava 36, Technotr 11, 119, Thomas Barwick 12, 119, Tinnapong 108, 127, Tom Chance 111, TomasSereda 23, 120, Traimak_Ivan 51, 78, 78, _Ultraforma_ 100, 126, Ulza 35, 121, Valentina Formaggi / 500px 48, 122, Vicente Soler / EyeEm 76, 124, Viktoriia Hnatiuk 51, 72, 75, Vincent Pommeyrol 83, 125, Vladimir Godnik 99, vm 102, Vstock LLC 44, Vuk8691 100, 126, Westend61 54, 35, 121, 35, 121, 71, 124, Xia Yuan 53, 53, Xjben 12, 119, Yasser Chalid 65, Yellow Dog Productions 80, 12, 119, Yongyuan 97, Zero Creatives 71, 124, Zoonar RF 28, 120; **PEARSON EDUCATION LTD:** Marcin Rosinski. Rafal Trubisz. Pearson Central Europe SP. Z.O.O. 53, 72, Trevor Clifford 7, 96, 118, WDG Photo 64, 123; **Shutterstock:** 28, 120, 1000 Words 96, 126, 123graphic 115, 151171 53, 3000ad 91, A. Mertens 59, 123, Ahturner 35, 121, AlbertMi 48, 122, Alec Taylor 48, 122, Aleksandr Lupin 35, 121, Alex Poison 23, 120, Alfa Photostudio 108, 127, Anastasios71 64, 123, Andrea Izzotti 48, Andrey Armyagov 90, Anna Jurkovska 12, 119, Antoniodiaz 87, ANURAK PONGPATIMET 48, 122, ArtMediaFactory 105, AustralianCamera 55, Avigator Fortuner 100, Basiczto 33, Bomshtein 80, Brenda Carson 49, Brocreative 88, 125, Canadastock 95, 126, Capricorn Studio 96, 126, Christian Delbert 112, 127, David Pereiras 118, Dmytro Vietrov 45, Elena Masiutkina 23, 120, Frenchwildlifephotograher 52, 122, Goodluz 88, 125, Graham Corney 115, Happy Together 89, Hung Chung Chih 53, Inc 35, 121, Inside Creative House 17, Irina Markova 55, Jan Fdz 64, 123, Luis Louro 18, 20, 30, 42, 54, 66, 78, 90, 102, 114, Jason McCartney 59, 123, JpegPhotographer 108, 127, Kdonmuang 84, 125, Kirsten Wahlquist 53, Kobby Dagan 53, Kues 7, 118, Kwangmoozaa 96, 126, Kwhw 48, LaKirr 64, 123, Leungchopan 52, 122, Lopolo 99, Luis Alonso Cardenas 64, 123, Luis Louro 18, 20, 30, 42, 54, 66, 78, 90, 102, 114, lunamarina 39, Martin Pelanek 53, 52, 122, MBI 56, Mentor57 84, 125, Mike Ver Sprill 79, Miroslav Chytil 53, Motive56 84, 125, Nadezda Murmakova 49, 47, 122, NAN728 59, 123, Nrqemi 95, 126, Oksana Trautwein 71, 124, Ondris 53, Patricia Hofmeester 28, 120, Paulaphoto 24, Peter Fodor 48, 122, Peter Stuckings 96, Prostock-studio 112, 127, Ranta Images 54, Richie Chan 96, RZ_Videos 48, Sakdawut Tangtongsap 23, 120, Samot 123, Samuel Borges Photography 101, Sean Pavone 95, 126, Sergey Uryadnikov 49, 53, Sirikorn Thamniyom 84, Solodovnik 83, 125, Stefan Lambauer 100, Steve Cukrov 108, 127, Stuart G Porter 49, Susan Carr 91, Syda Productions 54, 68, TaraPatta 112, 127, Targn Pleiades 96, 126, Tartalja 105, Testing 45, TinnaPong 40, 121, Troutnut 55, Uladzimir Zgurski 100, UnderTheSea 67, VasiliyBudarin 64, 123, Veronica Louro 36, Vichy Deal 101, Volodymyr TVERDOKHLIB 76, 124, Yupa Watchanakit 67, WDG Photo 64, 123, Yurakrasil 35, 121, Zoltan Major 48, 122: **Wikimedia Commons:** Diego Delso 101.

Illustrations
Andrea Castro Naranjo/Beehive Illustration pp. 18, 24, 66, 80; **JoJo Clinch/Plum Pudding** pp. 36, 44, 77, 81, 84, 93, 112, 114; **Emily Cooksey/Plum Pudding** (doodles & kid art); **Roger Stewart/Beehive Illustration** pp. 16 (Ex 2), 55, 60, 64, 65, 67 (ships), 68, 69; **Xiana Teimoy/Plum Pudding** pp. 12, 72, 108; **Diego Vaisberg/Advocate** pp. 8, 16 (Ex 1), 17, 20, 43, 67 (diagram), 79, 91, 103; **Laszlo Veres/Beehive Illustration** pp. 92, 104; **Lia Visirin/Advocate (course characters)**.

Cover illustrations © 2022 Disney Enterprises, Inc. All rights reserved. Pixar properties © Disney/Pixar

Copyright © 2022 Disney Enterprises, Inc. All rights reserved. Pixar properties © Disney/Pixar